# THE LEGEND OF KORRA

Created by
**BRYAN KONIETZKO**
**MICHAEL DANTE DiMARTINO**

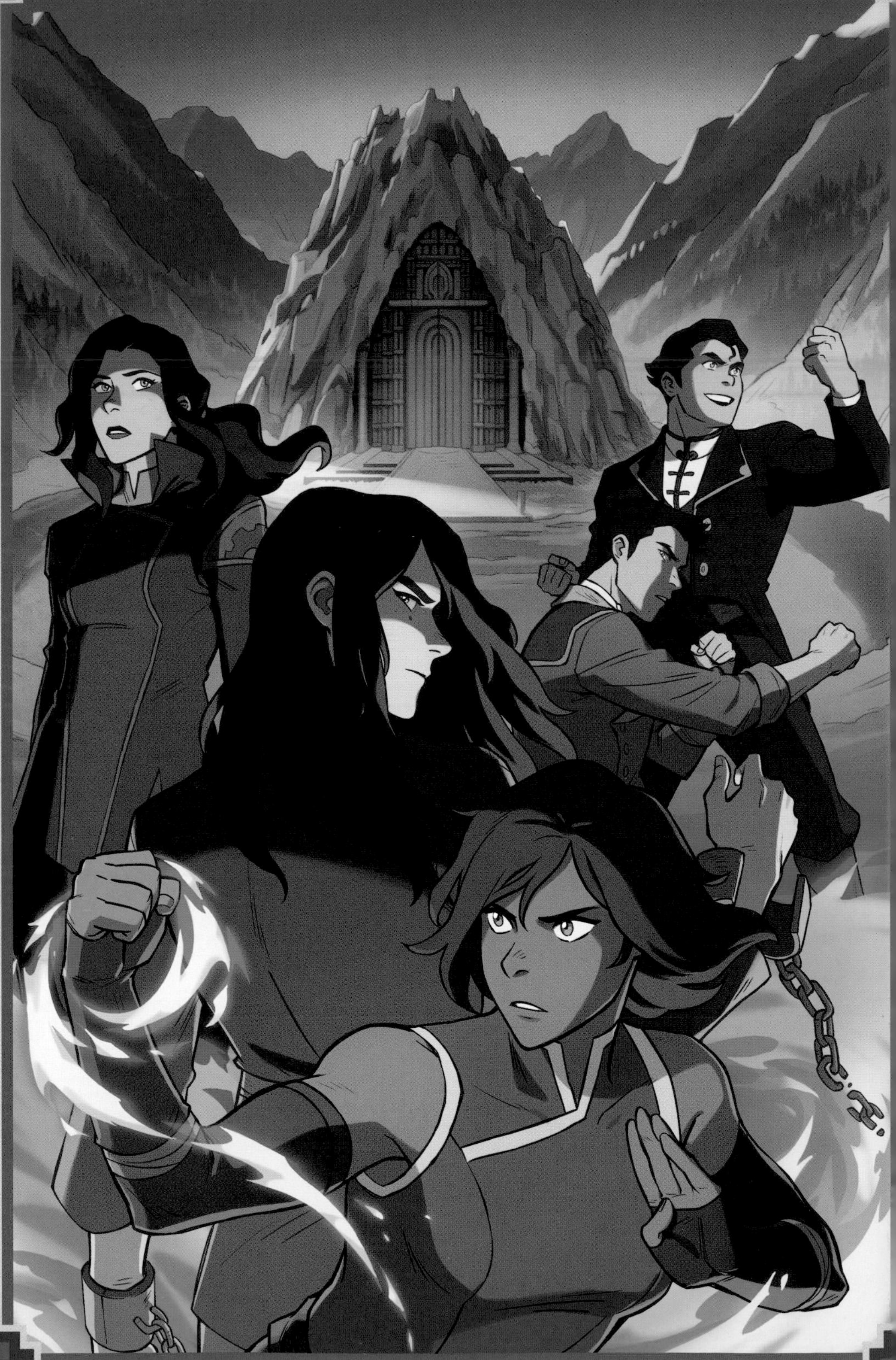

# THE LEGEND OF KORRA

## RUINS OF THE EMPIRE · PART ONE

written by
**MICHAEL DANTE DiMARTINO**

art by
**MICHELLE WONG**

colors by
**VIVIAN NG**

lettering by
**RACHEL DEERING**

cover by
**MICHELLE WONG** with **VIVIAN NG**

DARK HORSE BOOKS

president and publisher **MIKE RICHARDSON**

editors **DAVE MARSHALL** and **RACHEL ROBERTS**   assistant editor **JENNY BLENK**

designer **SARAH TERRY**   digital art technician **CHRISTIANNE GILLENARDO-GOUDREAU**

Special thanks to Linda Lee, Kat van Dam, James Salerno, and Joan Hilty
at Nickelodeon, and to Bryan Konietzko and Michael Dante DiMartino.

Published by **DARK HORSE BOOKS**
A division of Dark Horse Comics LLC.
10956 SE Main Street, Milwaukie, OR 97222

**DARKHORSE.COM** | **NICK.COM**

Comic Shop Locator Service: comicshoplocator.com

First edition: May 2019 | ISBN 978-1-50670-894-2

1 3 5 7 9 10 8 6 4 2
Printed in China

Neil Hankerson Executive Vice President • Tom Weddle Chief Financial Officer • Randy Stradley Vice
President of Publishing • Nick McWhorter Chief Business Development Officer • Dale LaFountain
Chief Information Officer • Matt Parkinson Vice President of Marketing • Cara Niece Vice President
of Production and Scheduling • Mark Bernardi Vice President of Book Trade and Digital Sales
• Ken Lizzi General Counsel • Dave Marshall Editor in Chief • Davey Estrada Editorial Director •
Chris Warner Senior Books Editor • Cary Grazzini Director of Specialty Projects • Lia Ribacchi Art
Director • Vanessa Todd-Holmes Director of Print Purchasing • Matt Dryer Director of Digital Art
and Prepress • Michael Gombos Senior Director of Licensed Publications • Kari Yadro Director of
Custom Programs • Kari Torson Director of International Licensing

Library of Congress Cataloging-in-Publication Data

Names: DiMartino, Michael Dante, writer, creator. | Wong, Michelle (Comic
  book artist), artist. | Ng, Vivian, colourist, artist. | Deering, Rachel,
  1983- letterer.
Title: The legend of Korra : ruins of the empire / written by Michael Dante
  DiMartino ; art by Michelle Wong ; colors by Vivian Ng ; lettering by
  Rachel Deering ; cover by Michelle Wong with Vivian Ng.
Other titles: Legend of Korra (Television program)
Description: Milwaukie, OR : Dark Horse Books, 2019- | "Created by Bryan
  Konietzko, Michael Dante DiMartino"
Identifiers: LCCN 2018052018 | ISBN 9781506708942 (part one : paperback)
Subjects: LCSH: Comic books, strips, etc. | BISAC: COMICS & GRAPHIC NOVELS /
  Media Tie-In. | COMICS & GRAPHIC NOVELS / Gay & Lesbian.
Classification: LCC PN6728.L434 D54 2019 | DDC 741.5/973--dc23
LC record available at https://lccn.loc.gov/2018052018

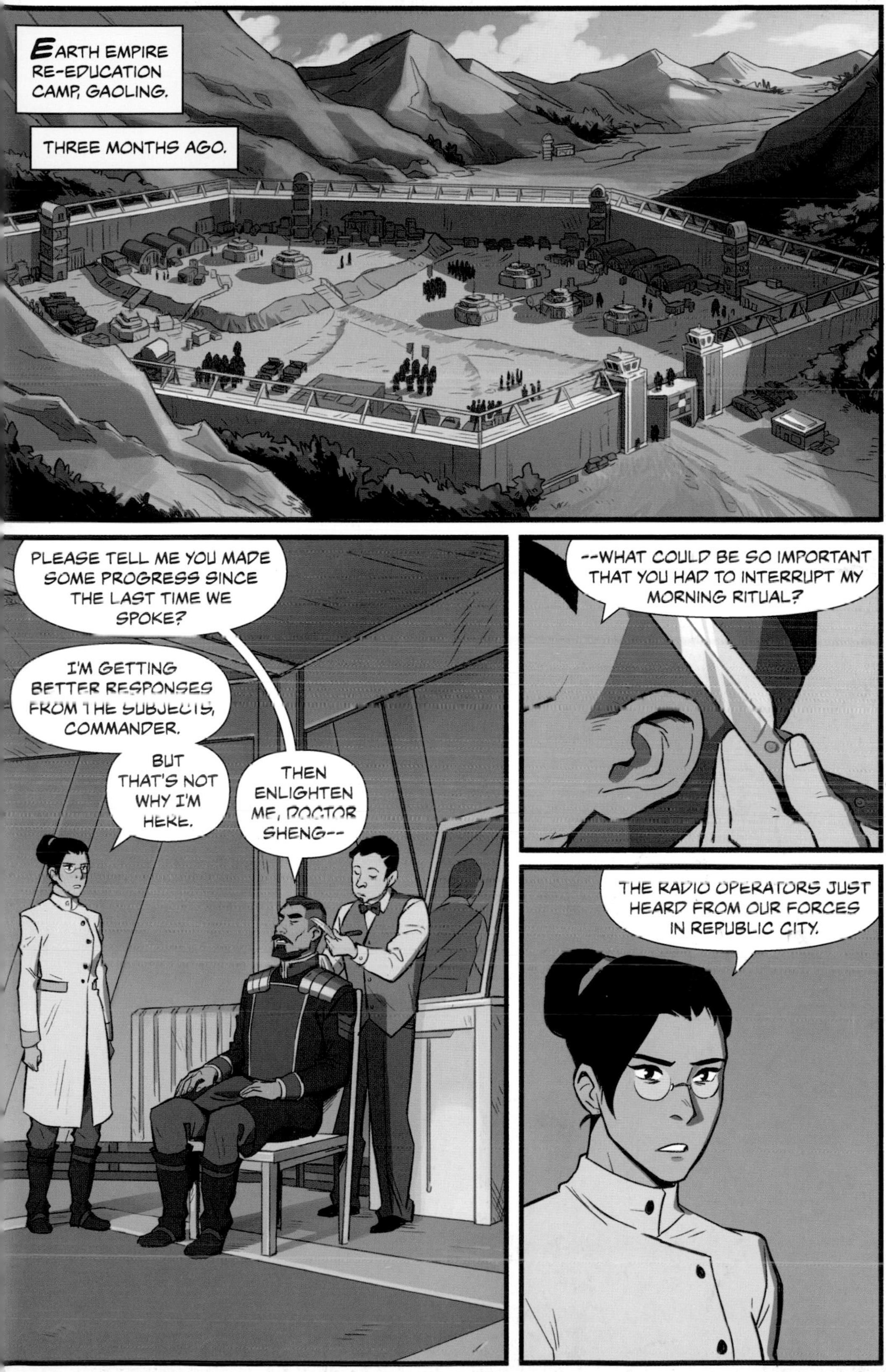
EARTH EMPIRE RE-EDUCATION CAMP, GAOLING.
THREE MONTHS AGO.
PLEASE TELL ME YOU MADE SOME PROGRESS SINCE THE LAST TIME WE SPOKE?
I'M GETTING BETTER RESPONSES FROM THE SUBJECTS, COMMANDER.
BUT THAT'S NOT WHY I'M HERE.
THEN ENLIGHTEN ME, DOCTOR SHENG--
--WHAT COULD BE SO IMPORTANT THAT YOU HAD TO INTERRUPT MY MORNING RITUAL?
THE RADIO OPERATORS JUST HEARD FROM OUR FORCES IN REPUBLIC CITY.

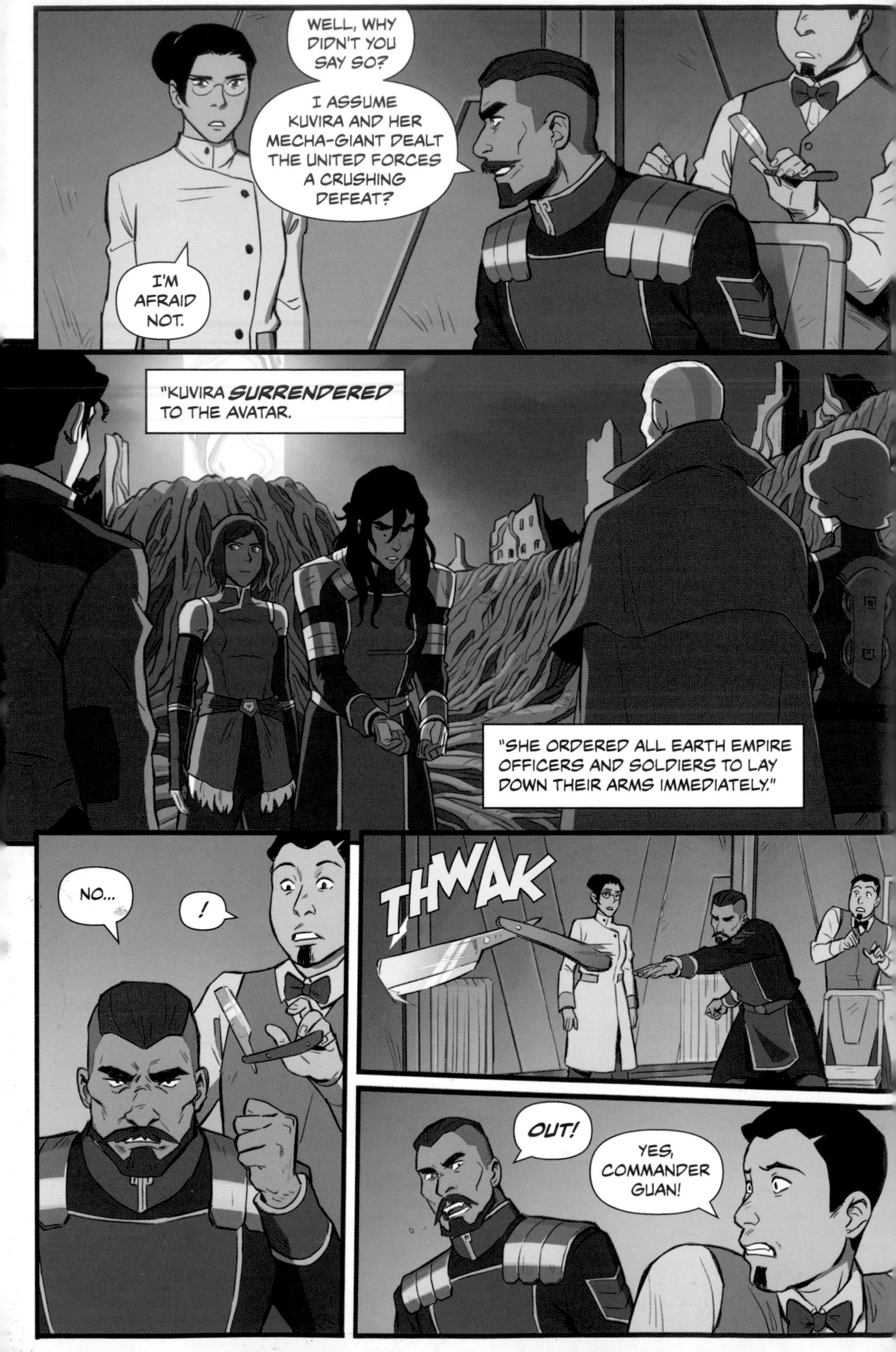
WELL, WHY DIDN'T YOU SAY SO?
I ASSUME KUVIRA AND HER MECHA-GIANT DEALT THE UNITED FORCES A CRUSHING DEFEAT?
I'M AFRAID NOT.
"KUVIRA SURRENDERED TO THE AVATAR.
"SHE ORDERED ALL EARTH EMPIRE OFFICERS AND SOLDIERS TO LAY DOWN THEIR ARMS IMMEDIATELY."
NO...
!
THWAK
OUT!
YES, COMMANDER GUAN!

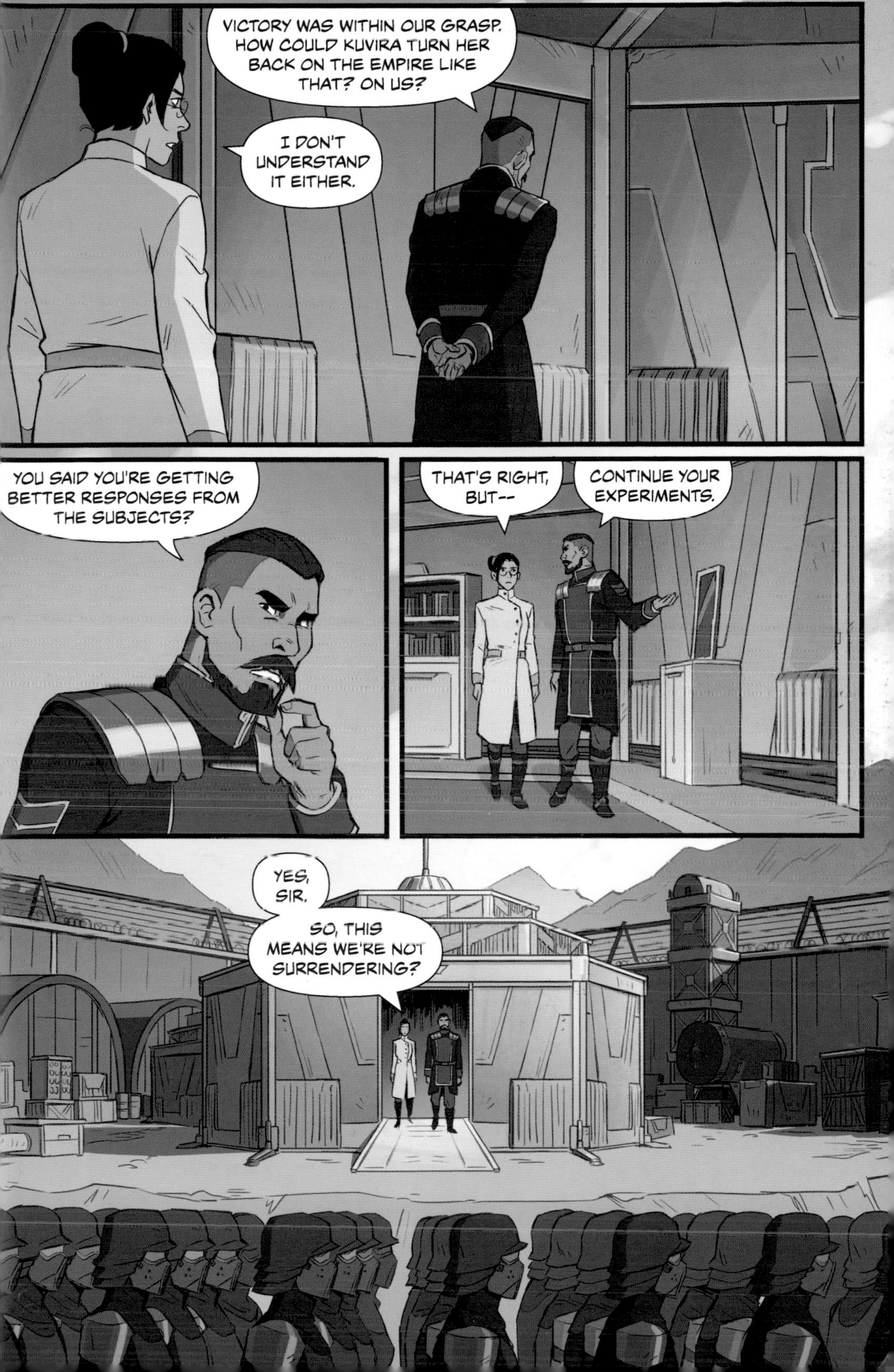
VICTORY WAS WITHIN OUR GRASP. HOW COULD KUVIRA TURN HER BACK ON THE EMPIRE LIKE THAT? ON US?
I DON'T UNDERSTAND IT EITHER.
YOU SAID YOU'RE GETTING BETTER RESPONSES FROM THE SUBJECTS?
THAT'S RIGHT, BUT--
CONTINUE YOUR EXPERIMENTS.
YES, SIR.
SO, THIS MEANS WE'RE NOT SURRENDERING?

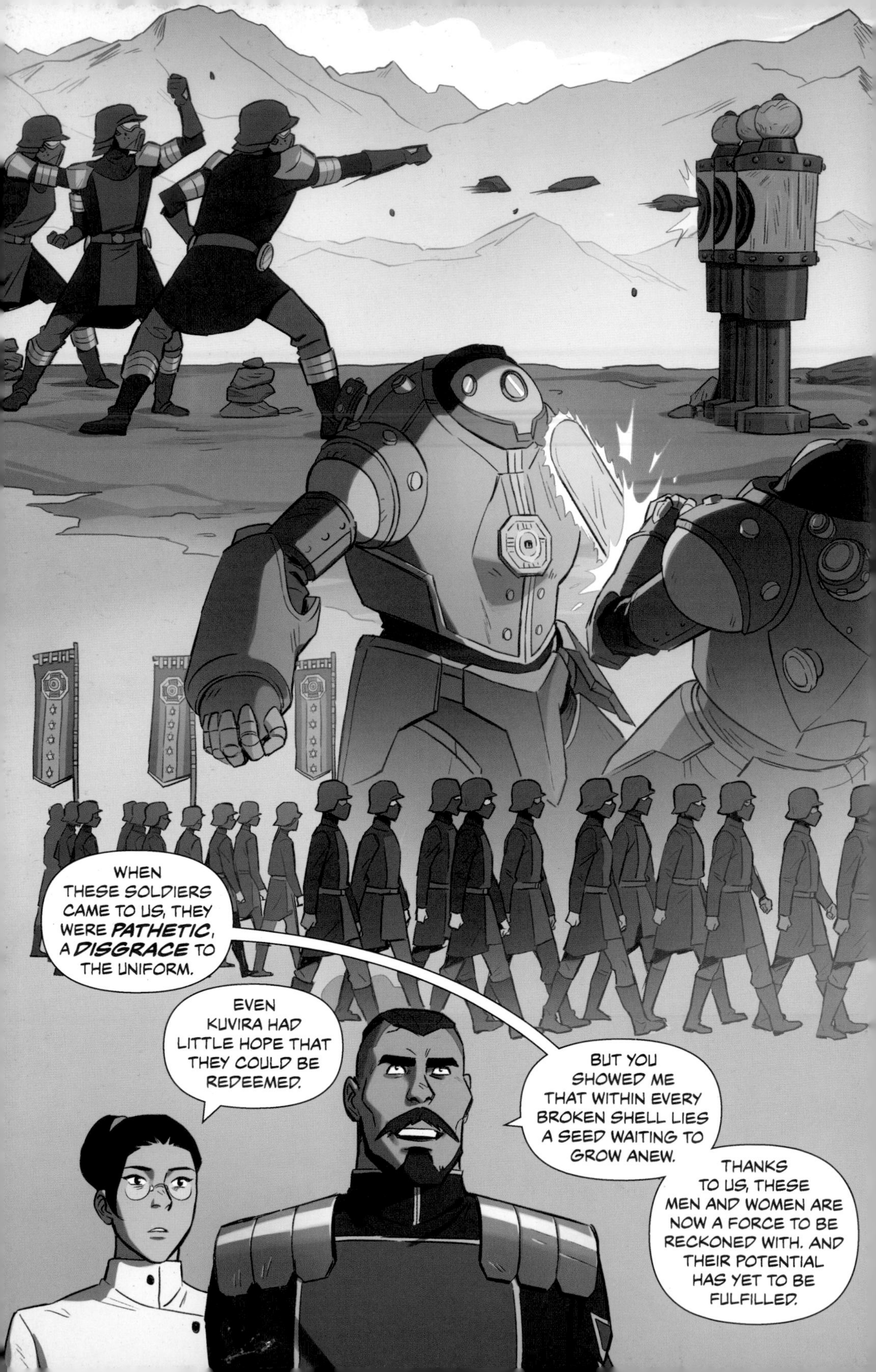
WHEN THESE SOLDIERS CAME TO US, THEY WERE ***PATHETIC***, A ***DISGRACE*** TO THE UNIFORM.
EVEN KUVIRA HAD LITTLE HOPE THAT THEY COULD BE REDEEMED.
BUT YOU SHOWED ME THAT WITHIN EVERY BROKEN SHELL LIES A SEED WAITING TO GROW ANEW.
THANKS TO US, THESE MEN AND WOMEN ARE NOW A FORCE TO BE RECKONED WITH. AND THEIR POTENTIAL HAS YET TO BE FULFILLED.

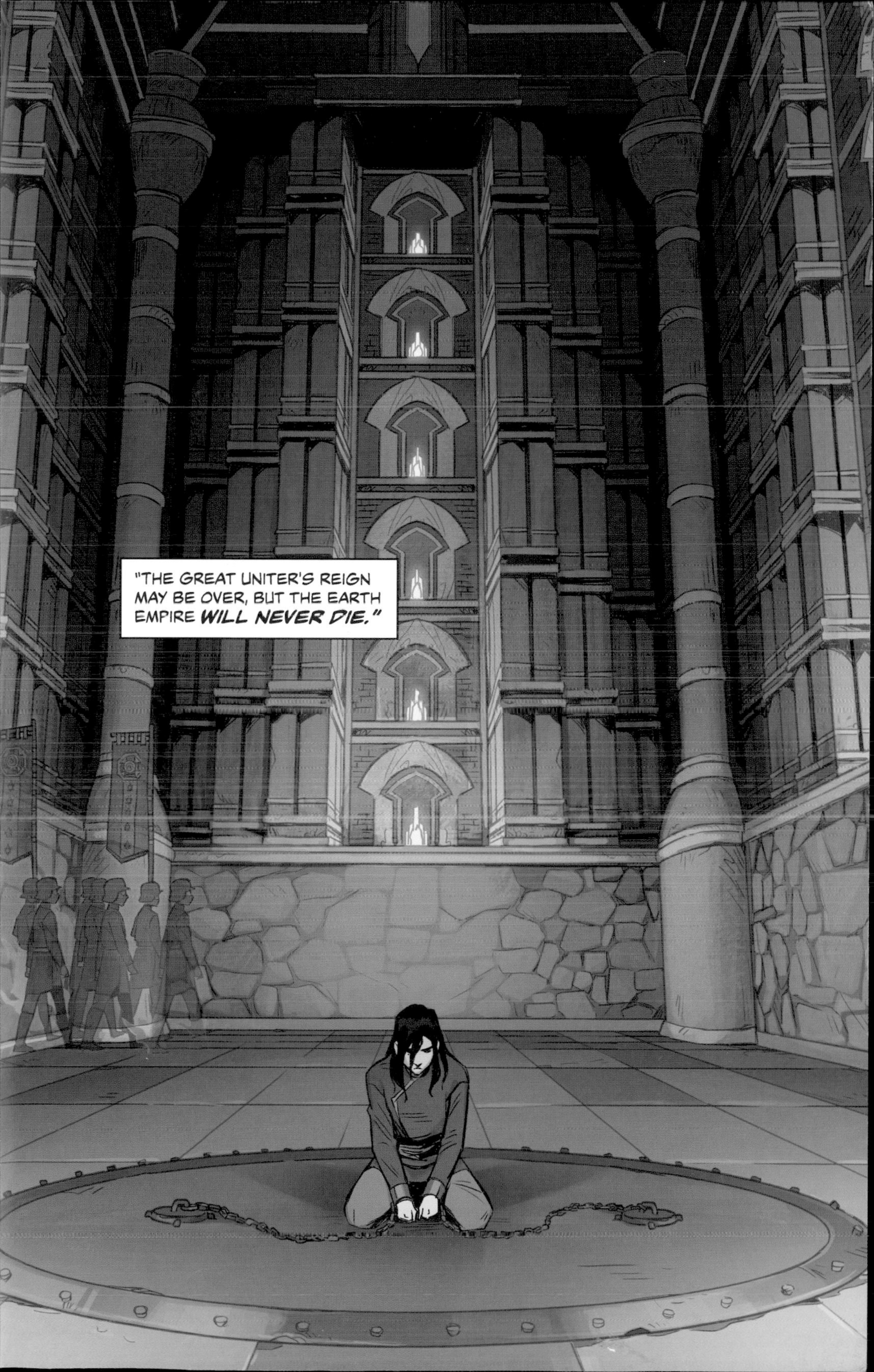
"THE GREAT UNITER'S REIGN MAY BE OVER, BUT THE EARTH EMPIRE **WILL NEVER DIE.**"

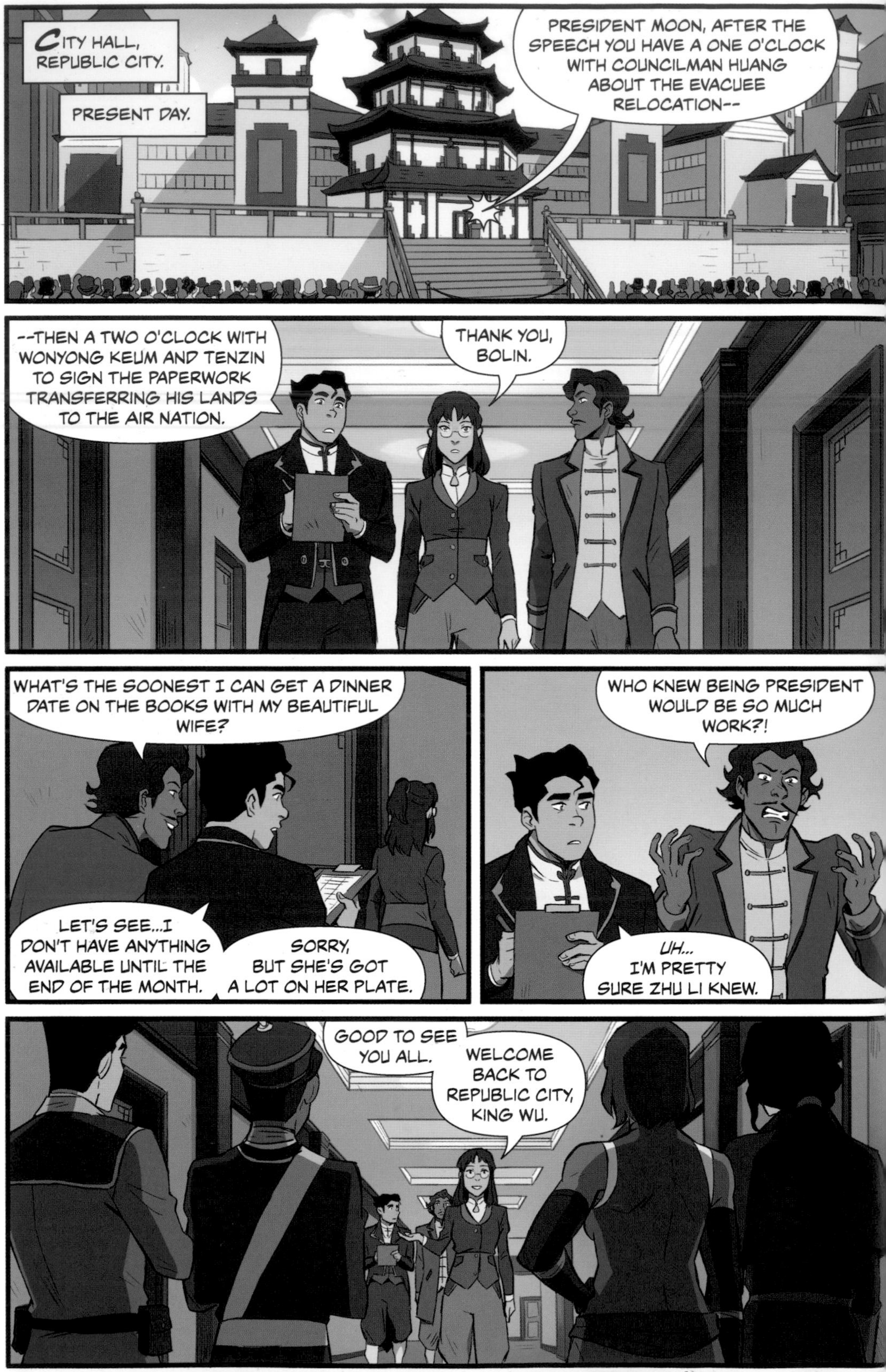
CITY HALL, REPUBLIC CITY.
PRESENT DAY.
PRESIDENT MOON, AFTER THE SPEECH YOU HAVE A ONE O'CLOCK WITH COUNCILMAN HUANG ABOUT THE EVACUEE RELOCATION--
--THEN A TWO O'CLOCK WITH WONYONG KEUM AND TENZIN TO SIGN THE PAPERWORK TRANSFERRING HIS LANDS TO THE AIR NATION.
THANK YOU, BOLIN.
WHAT'S THE SOONEST I CAN GET A DINNER DATE ON THE BOOKS WITH MY BEAUTIFUL WIFE?
LET'S SEE...I DON'T HAVE ANYTHING AVAILABLE UNTIL THE END OF THE MONTH.
SORRY, BUT SHE'S GOT A LOT ON HER PLATE.
WHO KNEW BEING PRESIDENT WOULD BE SO MUCH WORK?!
UH... I'M PRETTY SURE ZHU LI KNEW.
GOOD TO SEE YOU ALL.
WELCOME BACK TO REPUBLIC CITY, KING WU.

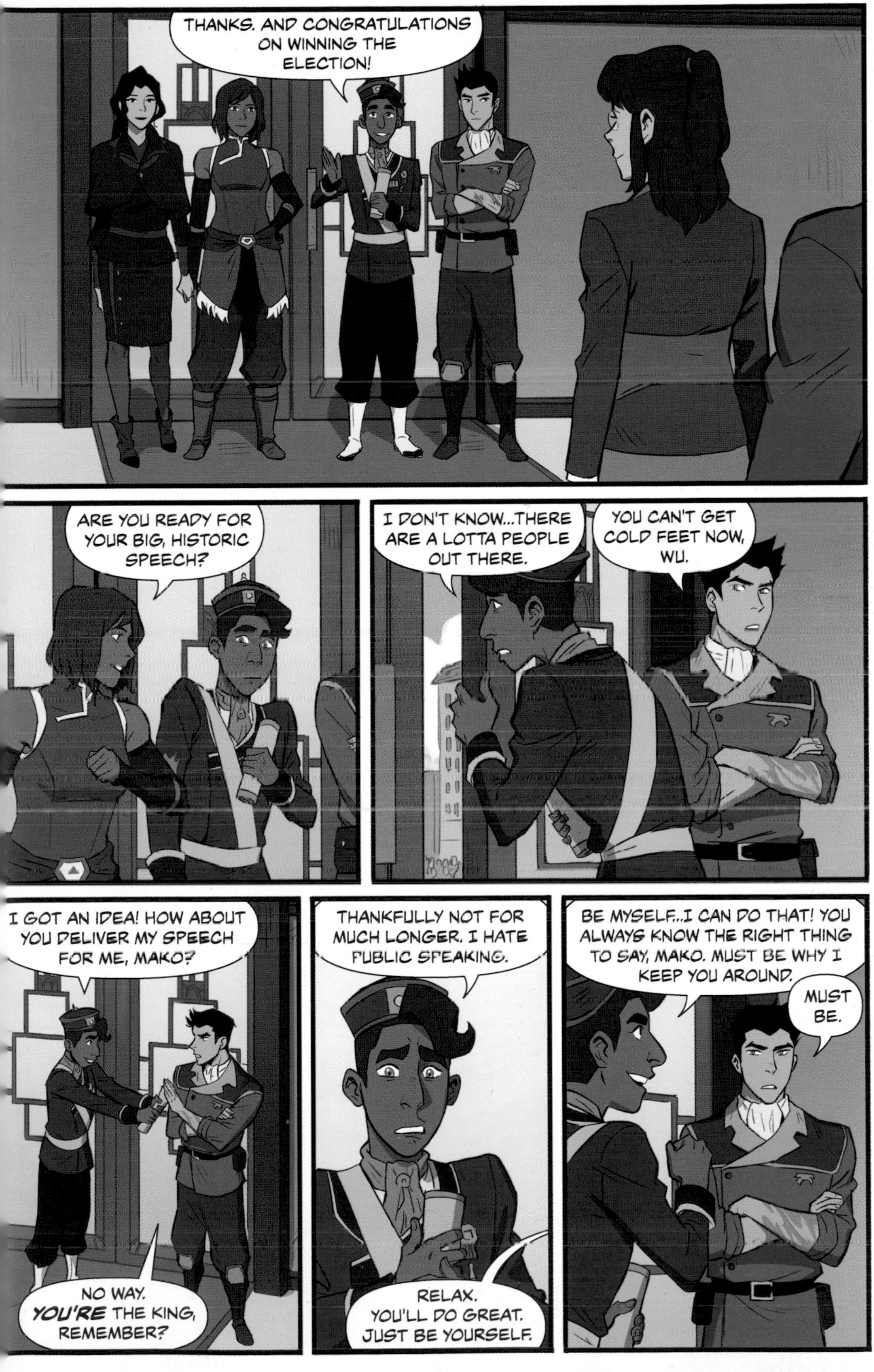
THANKS. AND CONGRATULATIONS ON WINNING THE ELECTION!
ARE YOU READY FOR YOUR BIG, HISTORIC SPEECH?
I DON'T KNOW...THERE ARE A LOTTA PEOPLE OUT THERE.
YOU CAN'T GET COLD FEET NOW, WU.
I GOT AN IDEA! HOW ABOUT YOU DELIVER MY SPEECH FOR ME, MAKO?
NO WAY. *YOU'RE* THE KING, REMEMBER?
THANKFULLY NOT FOR MUCH LONGER. I HATE PUBLIC SPEAKING.
RELAX. YOU'LL DO GREAT. JUST BE YOURSELF.
BE MYSELF...I CAN DO THAT! YOU ALWAYS KNOW THE RIGHT THING TO SAY, MAKO. MUST BE WHY I KEEP YOU AROUND.
MUST BE.

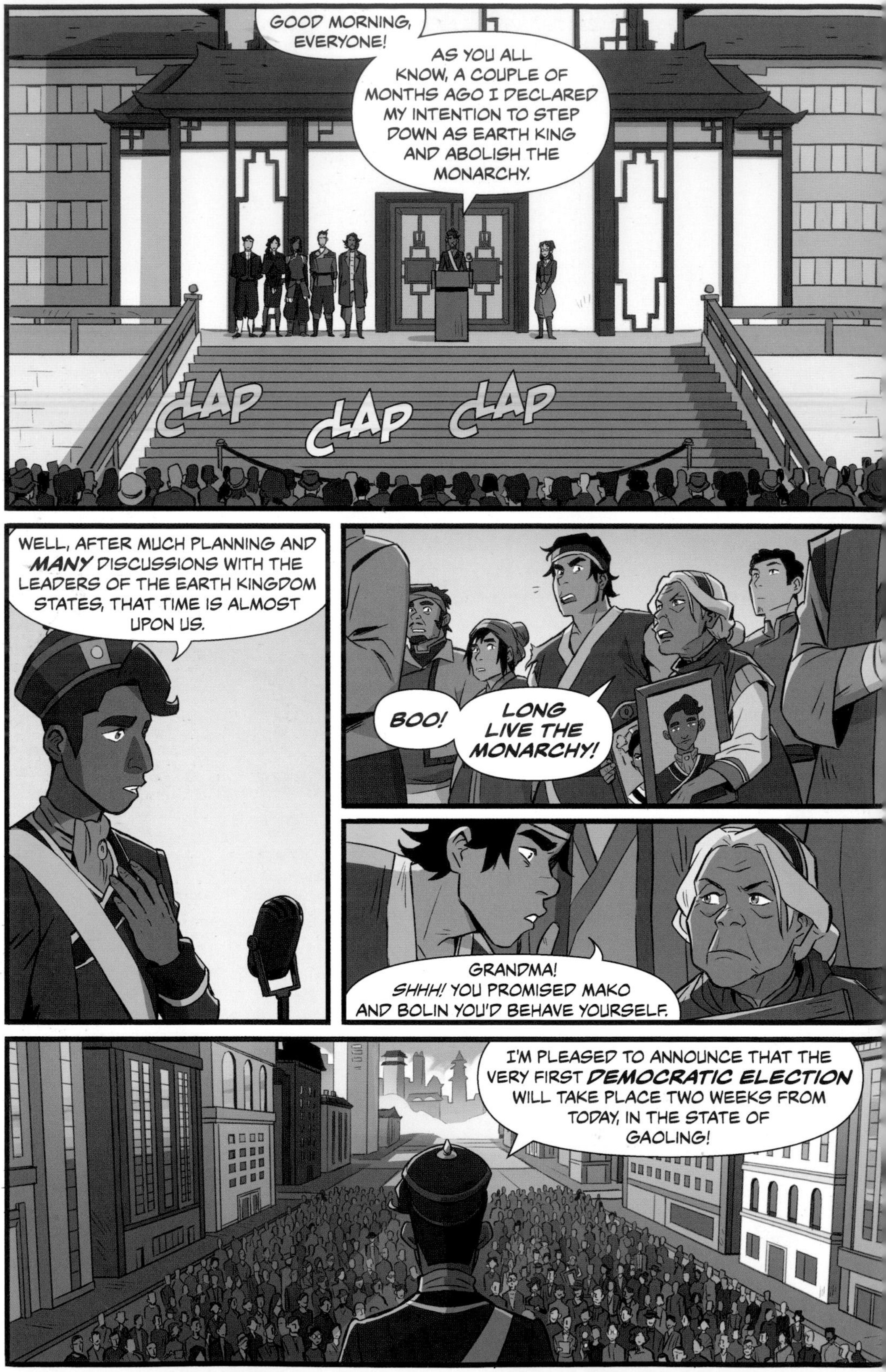
GOOD MORNING, EVERYONE!
AS YOU ALL KNOW, A COUPLE OF MONTHS AGO I DECLARED MY INTENTION TO STEP DOWN AS EARTH KING AND ABOLISH THE MONARCHY.
CLAP CLAP CLAP
WELL, AFTER MUCH PLANNING AND MANY DISCUSSIONS WITH THE LEADERS OF THE EARTH KINGDOM STATES, THAT TIME IS ALMOST UPON US.
BOO!
LONG LIVE THE MONARCHY!
GRANDMA! SHHH! YOU PROMISED MAKO AND BOLIN YOU'D BEHAVE YOURSELF.
I'M PLEASED TO ANNOUNCE THAT THE VERY FIRST DEMOCRATIC ELECTION WILL TAKE PLACE TWO WEEKS FROM TODAY, IN THE STATE OF GAOLING!

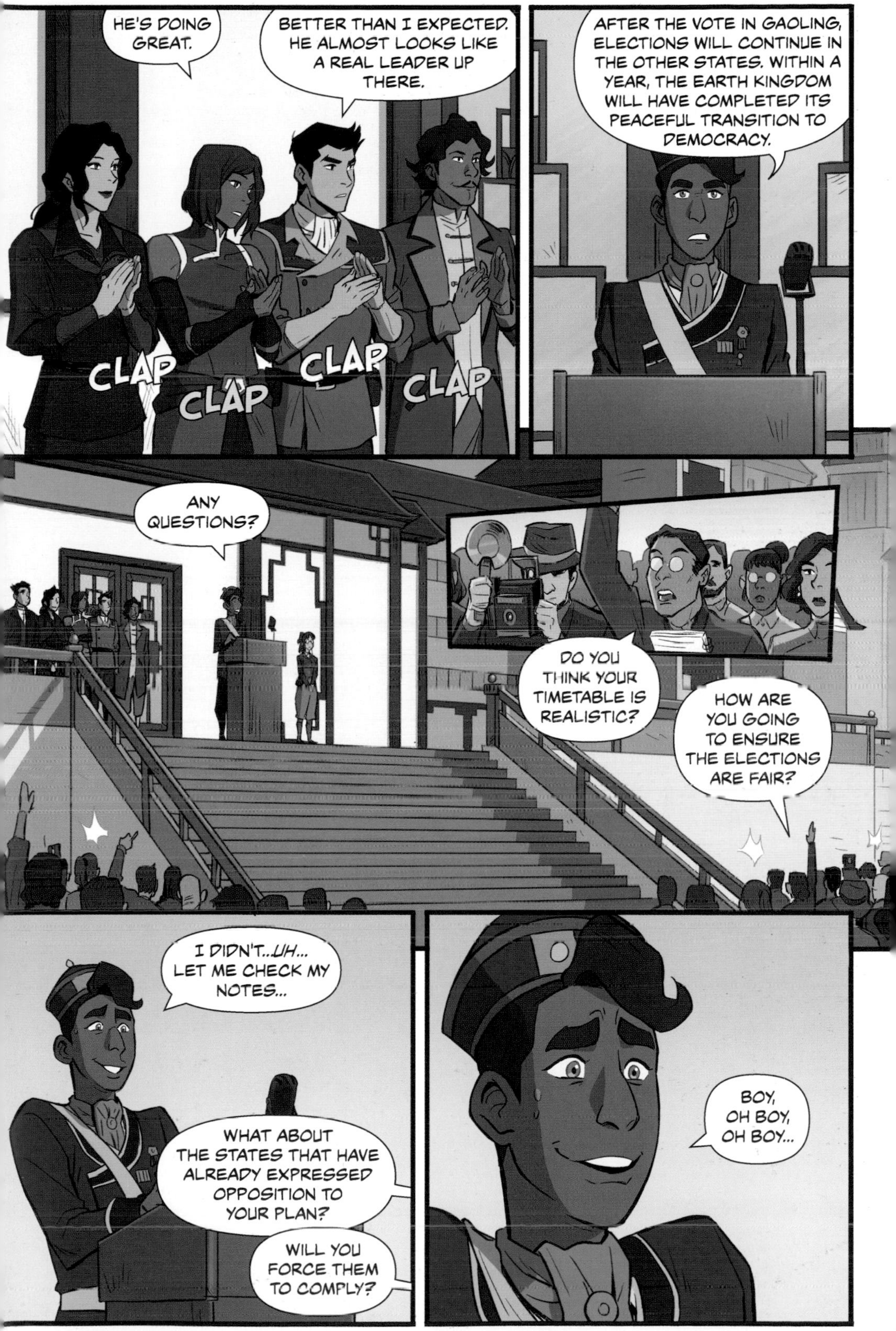
HE'S DOING GREAT.
BETTER THAN I EXPECTED. HE ALMOST LOOKS LIKE A REAL LEADER UP THERE.
CLAP
CLAP
CLAP
CLAP
AFTER THE VOTE IN GAOLING, ELECTIONS WILL CONTINUE IN THE OTHER STATES. WITHIN A YEAR, THE EARTH KINGDOM WILL HAVE COMPLETED ITS PEACEFUL TRANSITION TO DEMOCRACY.
ANY QUESTIONS?
DO YOU THINK YOUR TIMETABLE IS REALISTIC?
HOW ARE YOU GOING TO ENSURE THE ELECTIONS ARE FAIR?
I DIDN'T...UH... LET ME CHECK MY NOTES...
WHAT ABOUT THE STATES THAT HAVE ALREADY EXPRESSED OPPOSITION TO YOUR PLAN?
WILL YOU FORCE THEM TO COMPLY?
BOY, OH BOY, OH BOY...

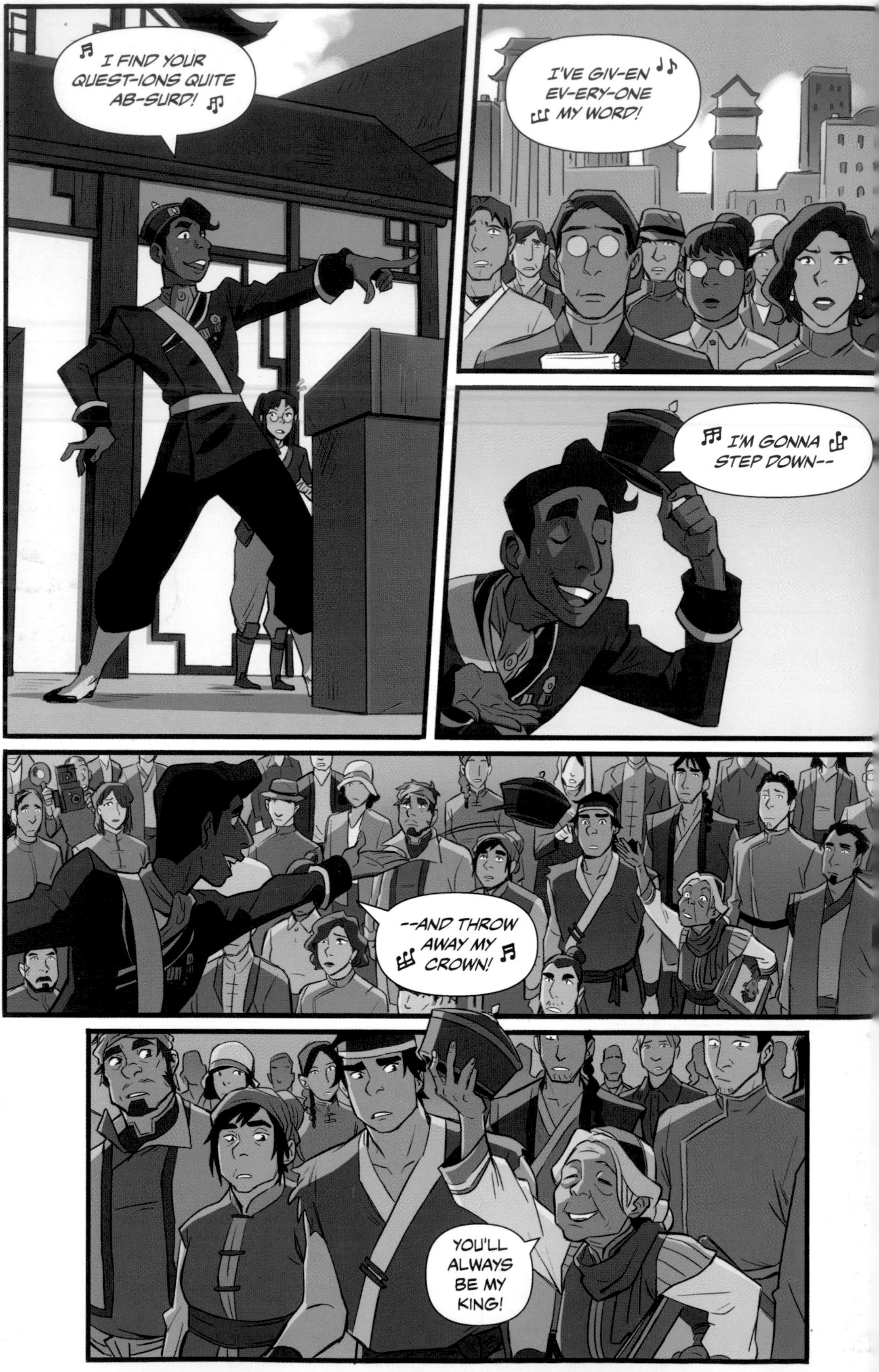
I FIND YOUR QUEST-IONS QUITE AB-SURD!
I'VE GIV-EN EV-ERY-ONE MY WORD!
I'M GONNA STEP DOWN--
--AND THROW AWAY MY CROWN!
YOU'LL ALWAYS BE MY KING!

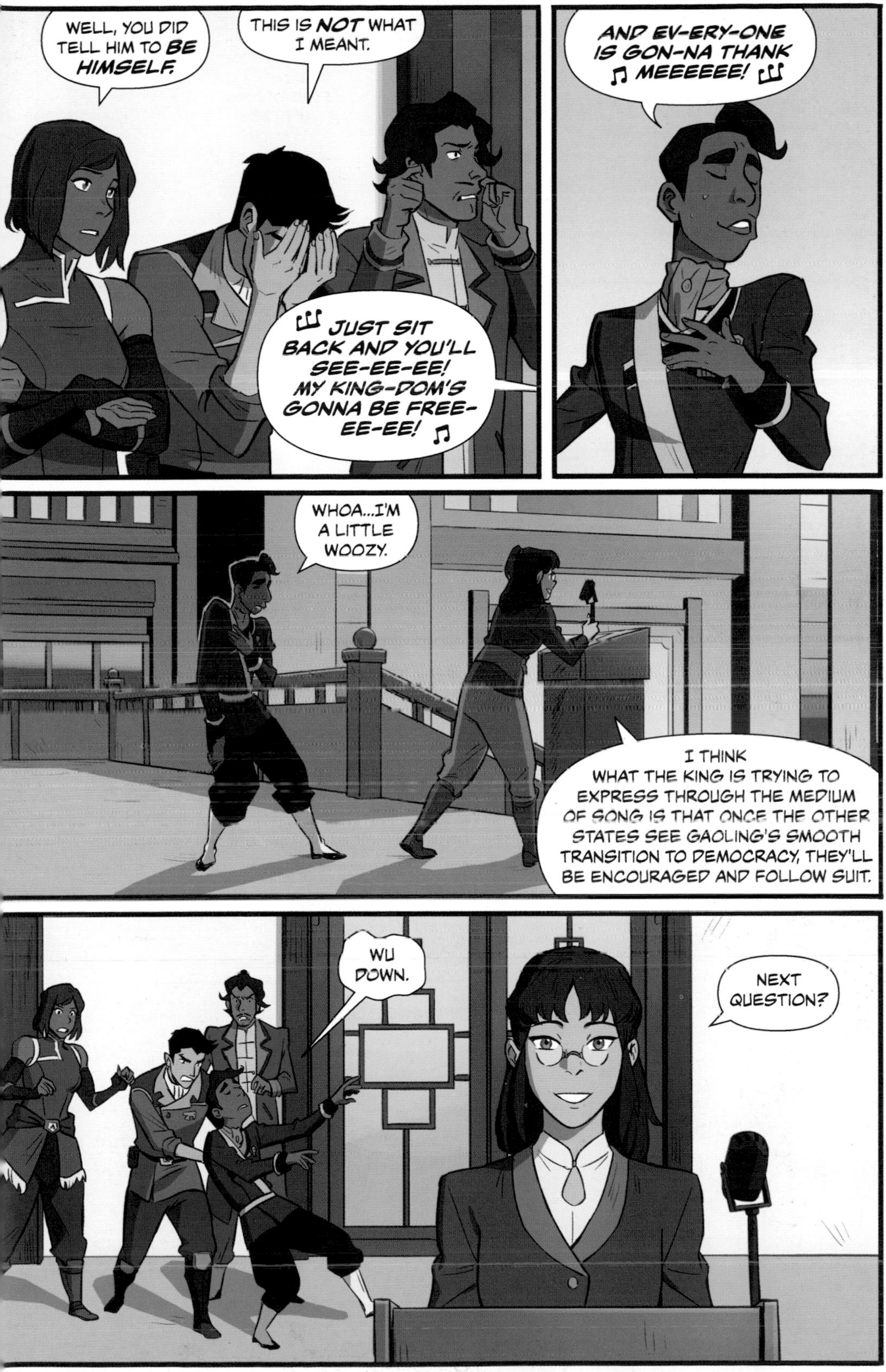
WELL, YOU DID TELL HIM TO BE HIMSELF.
THIS IS NOT WHAT I MEANT.
JUST SIT BACK AND YOU'LL SEE-EE-EE! MY KING-DOM'S GONNA BE FREE-EE-EE!
AND EV-ERY-ONE IS GON-NA THANK MEEEEEE!
WHOA...I'M A LITTLE WOOZY.
I THINK WHAT THE KING IS TRYING TO EXPRESS THROUGH THE MEDIUM OF SONG IS THAT ONCE THE OTHER STATES SEE GAOLING'S SMOOTH TRANSITION TO DEMOCRACY, THEY'LL BE ENCOURAGED AND FOLLOW SUIT.
WU DOWN.
NEXT QUESTION?

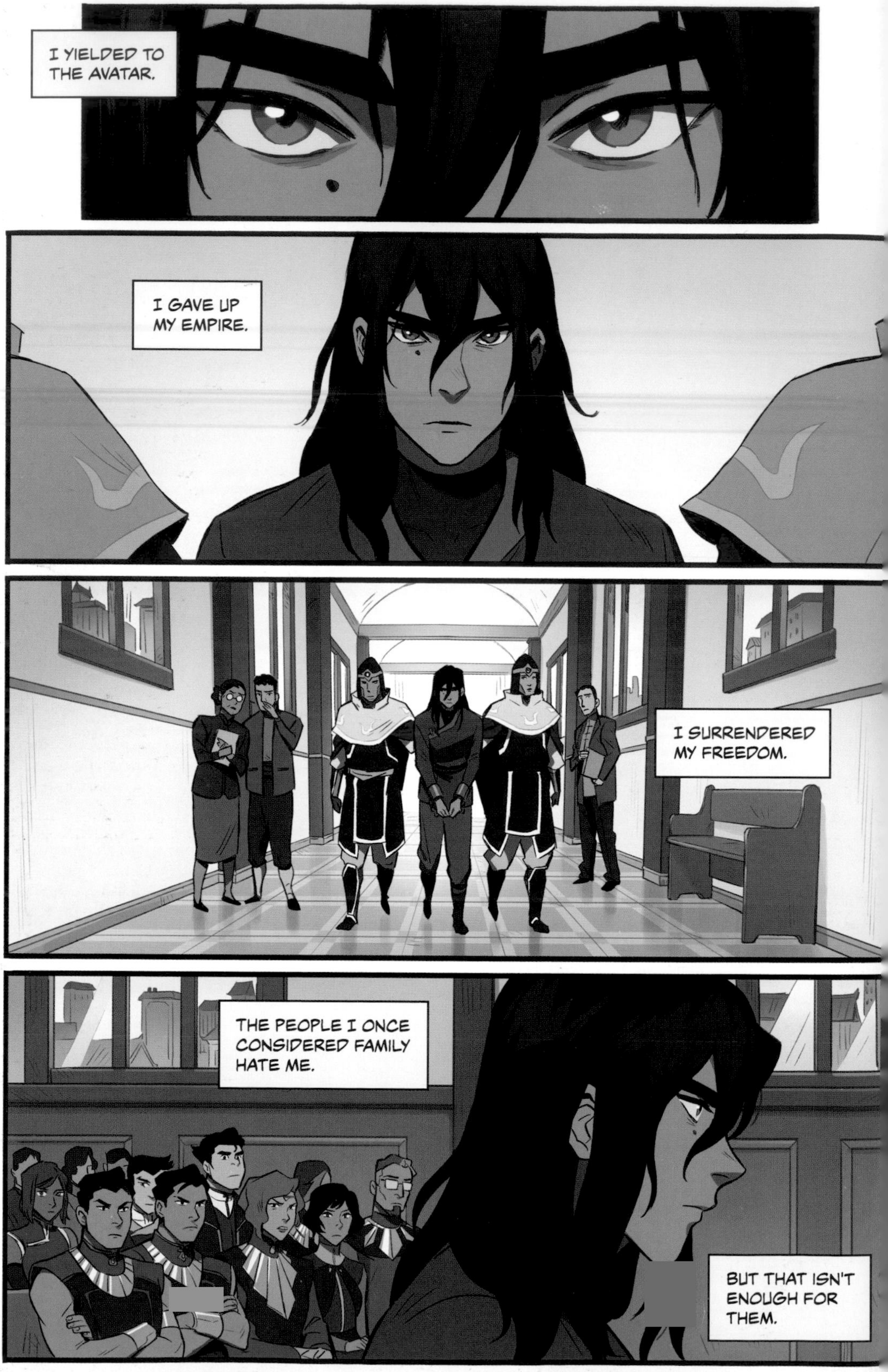
I YIELDED TO THE AVATAR.
I GAVE UP MY EMPIRE.
I SURRENDERED MY FREEDOM.
THE PEOPLE I ONCE CONSIDERED FAMILY HATE ME.
BUT THAT ISN'T ENOUGH FOR THEM.

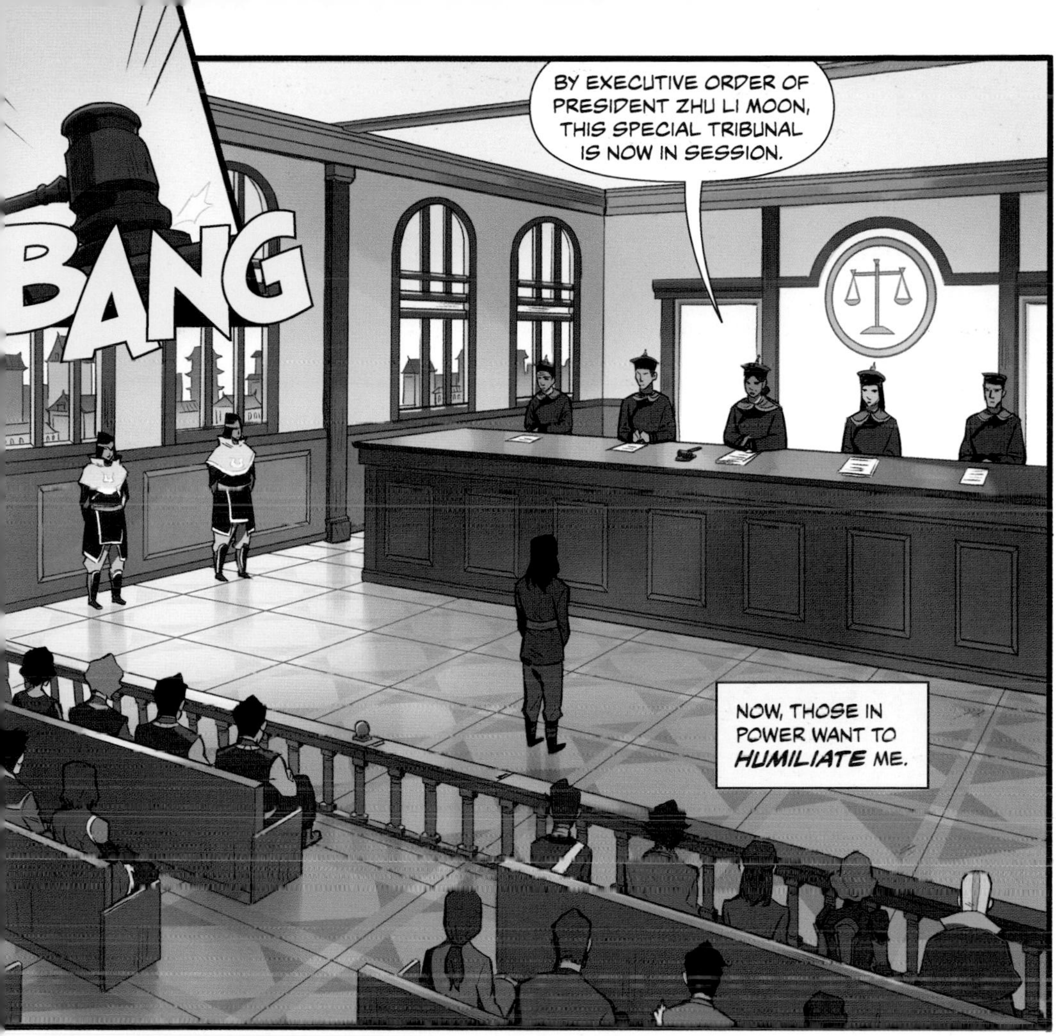
BANG
BY EXECUTIVE ORDER OF PRESIDENT ZHU LI MOON, THIS SPECIAL TRIBUNAL IS NOW IN SESSION.
NOW, THOSE IN POWER WANT TO *HUMILIATE* ME.

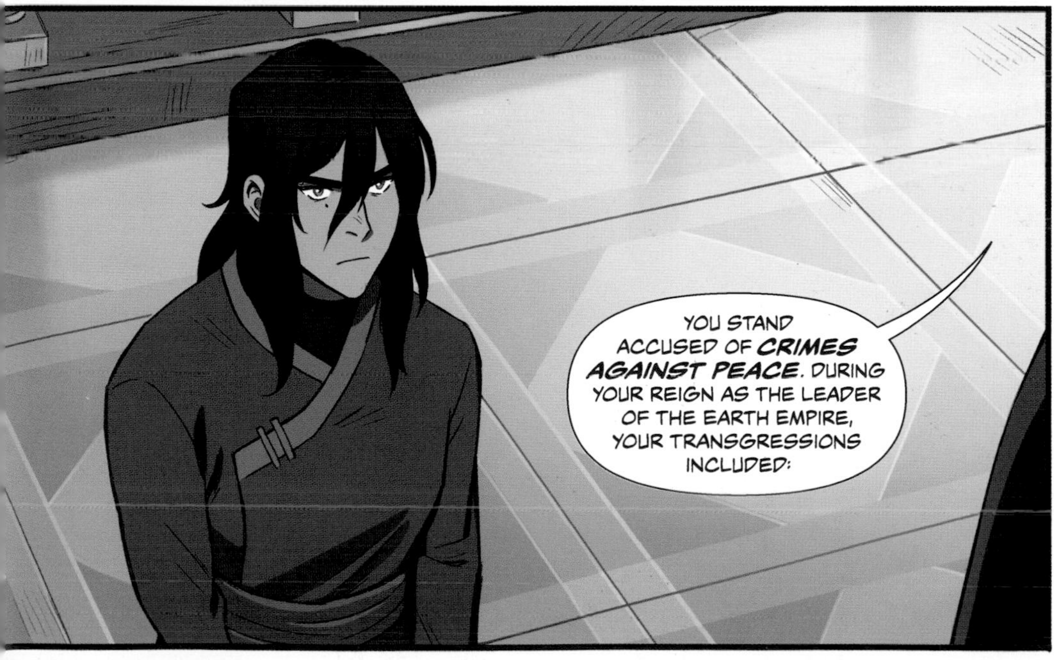
YOU STAND ACCUSED OF *CRIMES AGAINST PEACE*. DURING YOUR REIGN AS THE LEADER OF THE EARTH EMPIRE, YOUR TRANSGRESSIONS INCLUDED:

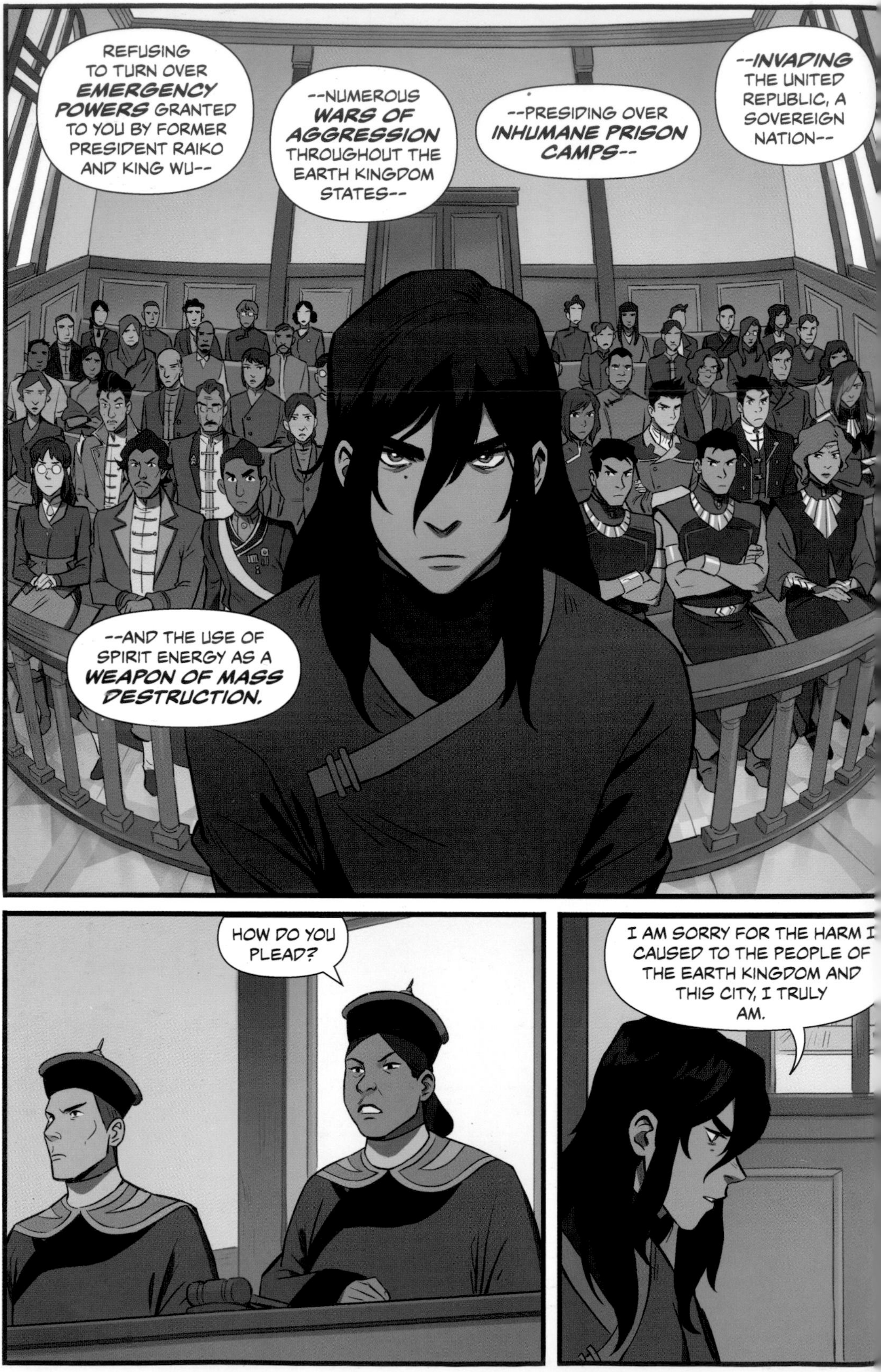
REFUSING TO TURN OVER EMERGENCY POWERS GRANTED TO YOU BY FORMER PRESIDENT RAIKO AND KING WU--
--NUMEROUS WARS OF AGGRESSION THROUGHOUT THE EARTH KINGDOM STATES--
--PRESIDING OVER INHUMANE PRISON CAMPS--
--INVADING THE UNITED REPUBLIC, A SOVEREIGN NATION--
--AND THE USE OF SPIRIT ENERGY AS A WEAPON OF MASS DESTRUCTION.
HOW DO YOU PLEAD?
I AM SORRY FOR THE HARM I CAUSED TO THE PEOPLE OF THE EARTH KINGDOM AND THIS CITY, I TRULY AM.

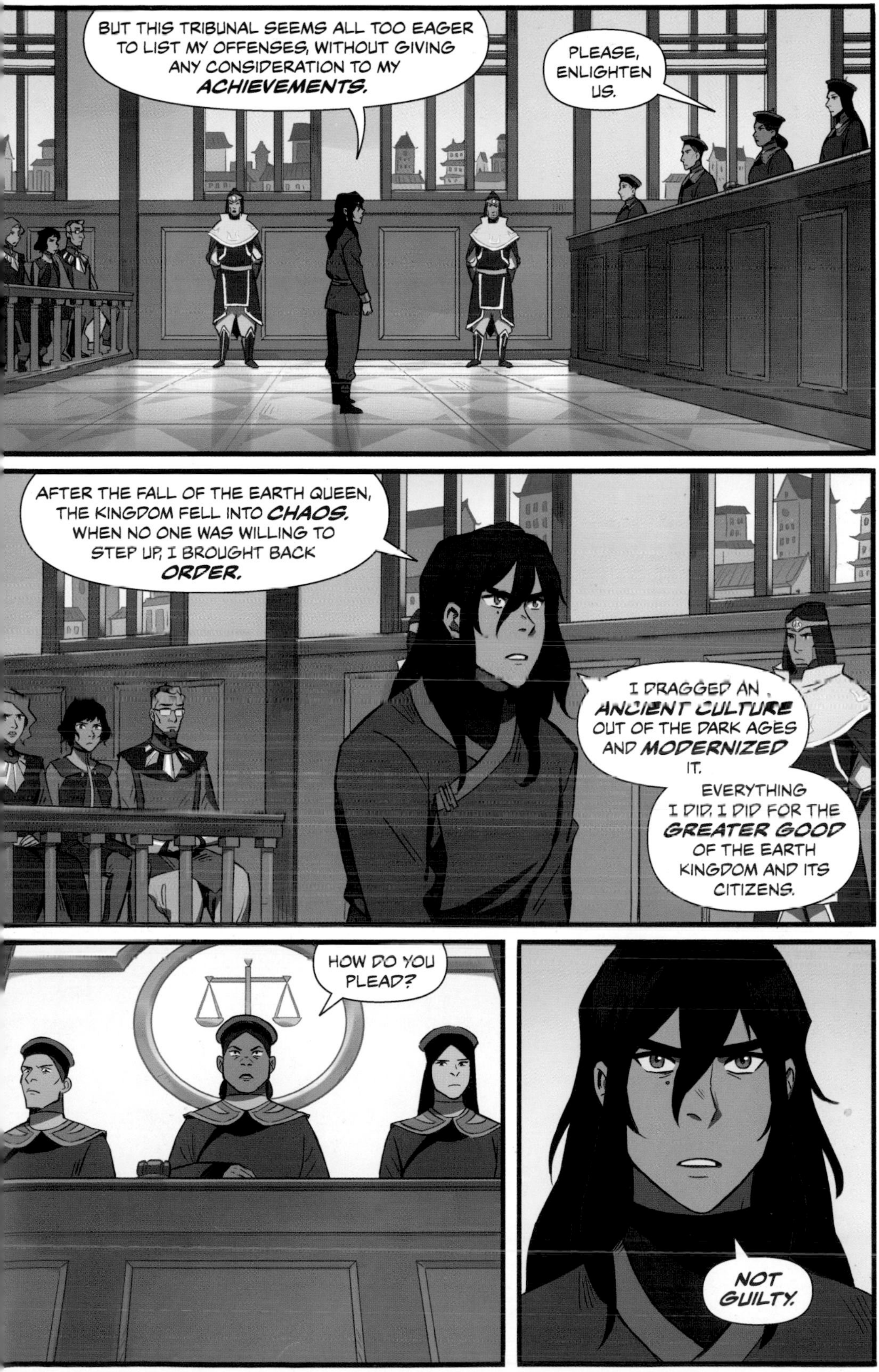
BUT THIS TRIBUNAL SEEMS ALL TOO EAGER TO LIST MY OFFENSES, WITHOUT GIVING ANY CONSIDERATION TO MY ACHIEVEMENTS.
PLEASE, ENLIGHTEN US.
AFTER THE FALL OF THE EARTH QUEEN, THE KINGDOM FELL INTO CHAOS. WHEN NO ONE WAS WILLING TO STEP UP, I BROUGHT BACK ORDER.
I DRAGGED AN ANCIENT CULTURE OUT OF THE DARK AGES AND MODERNIZED IT.
EVERYTHING I DID, I DID FOR THE GREATER GOOD OF THE EARTH KINGDOM AND ITS CITIZENS.
HOW DO YOU PLEAD?
NOT GUILTY.

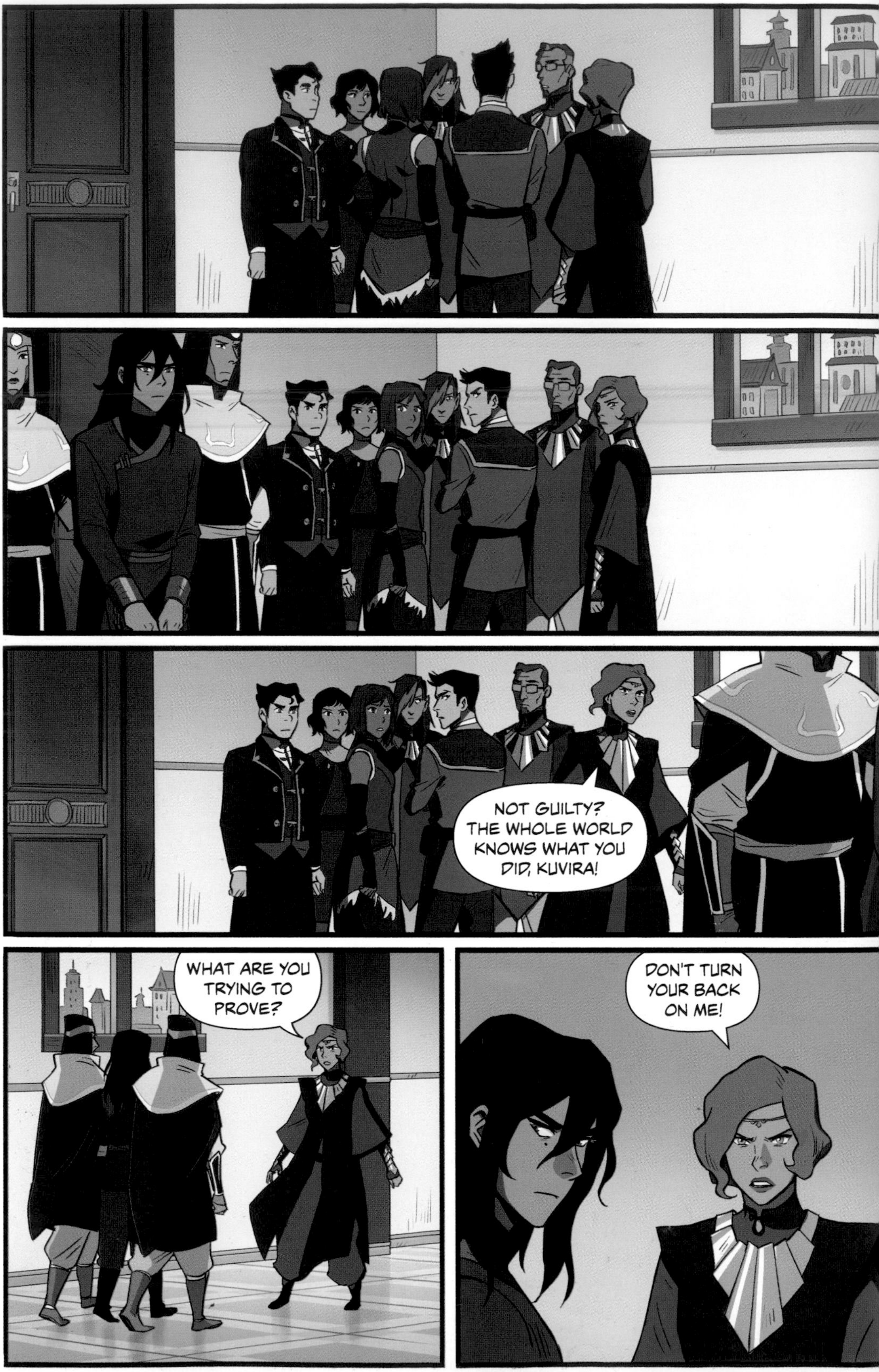
NOT GUILTY? THE WHOLE WORLD KNOWS WHAT YOU DID, KUVIRA!
WHAT ARE YOU TRYING TO PROVE?
DON'T TURN YOUR BACK ON ME!

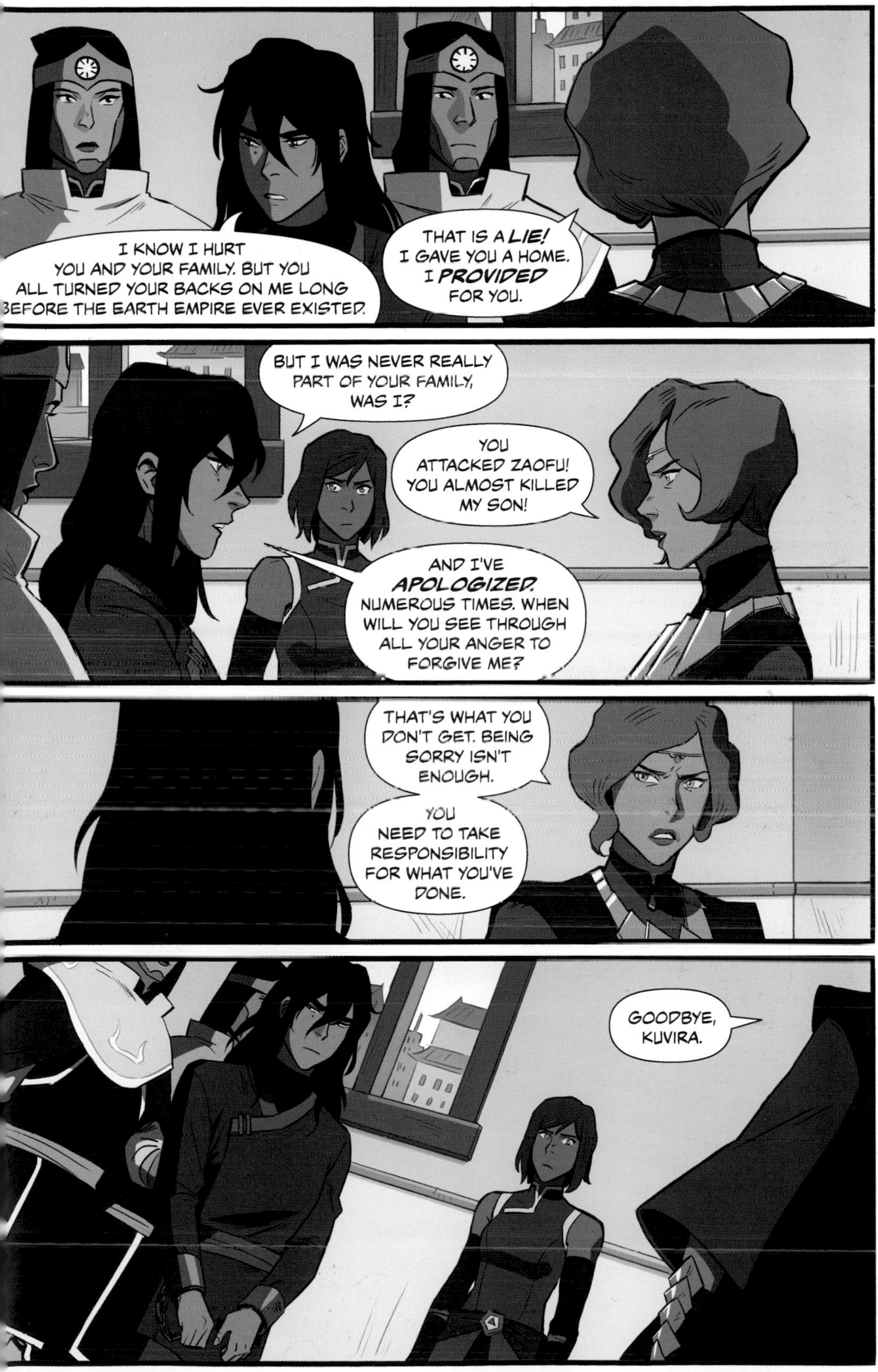
I KNOW I HURT YOU AND YOUR FAMILY. BUT YOU ALL TURNED YOUR BACKS ON ME LONG BEFORE THE EARTH EMPIRE EVER EXISTED.
THAT IS A LIE! I GAVE YOU A HOME. I PROVIDED FOR YOU.
BUT I WAS NEVER REALLY PART OF YOUR FAMILY, WAS I?
YOU ATTACKED ZAOFU! YOU ALMOST KILLED MY SON!
AND I'VE APOLOGIZED. NUMEROUS TIMES. WHEN WILL YOU SEE THROUGH ALL YOUR ANGER TO FORGIVE ME?
THAT'S WHAT YOU DON'T GET. BEING SORRY ISN'T ENOUGH.
YOU NEED TO TAKE RESPONSIBILITY FOR WHAT YOU'VE DONE.
GOODBYE, KUVIRA.

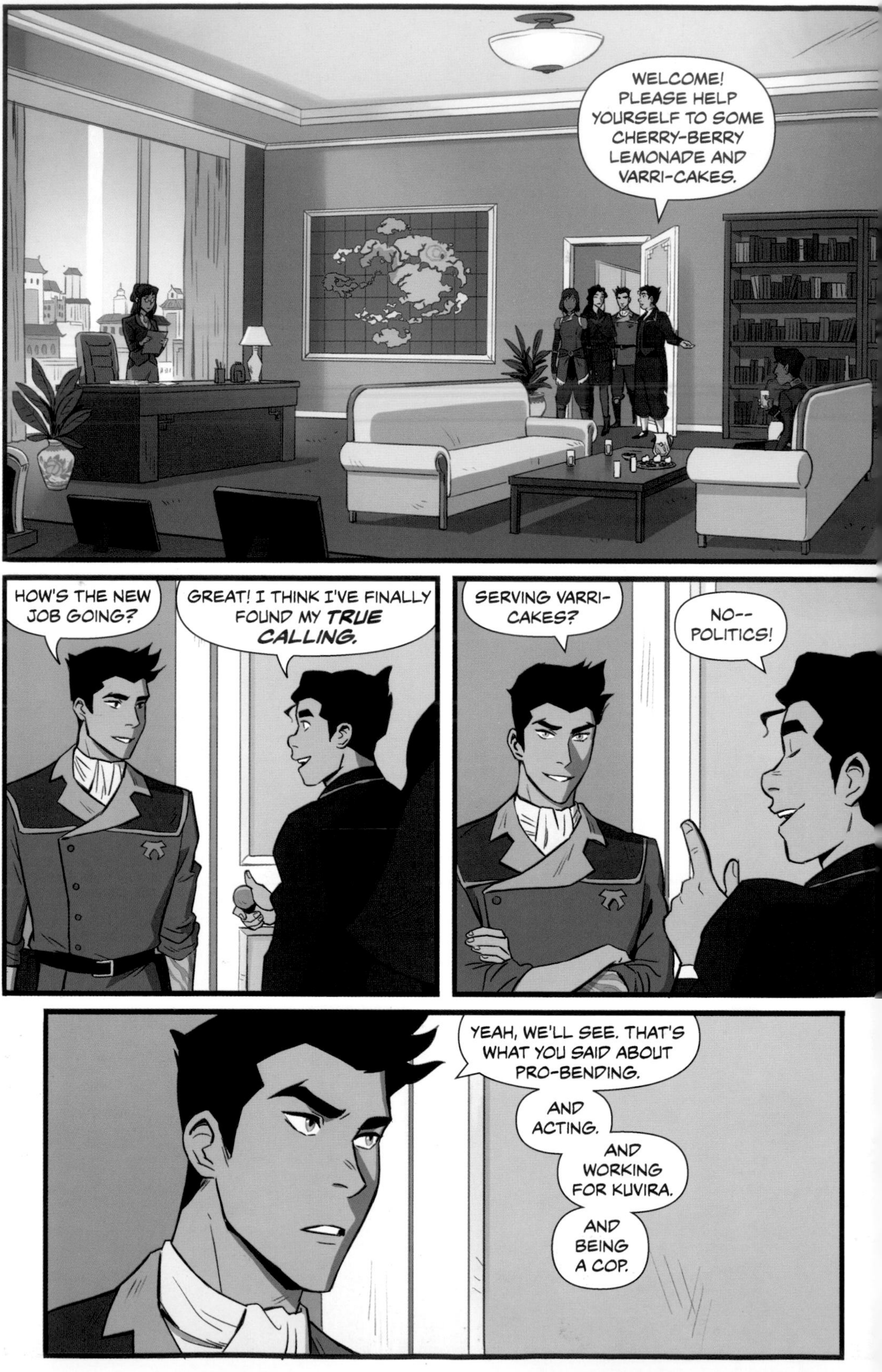
WELCOME! PLEASE HELP YOURSELF TO SOME CHERRY-BERRY LEMONADE AND VARRI-CAKES.
HOW'S THE NEW JOB GOING?
GREAT! I THINK I'VE FINALLY FOUND MY TRUE CALLING.
SERVING VARRI-CAKES?
NO-- POLITICS!
YEAH, WE'LL SEE. THAT'S WHAT YOU SAID ABOUT PRO-BENDING.
AND ACTING.
AND WORKING FOR KUVIRA.
AND BEING A COP.

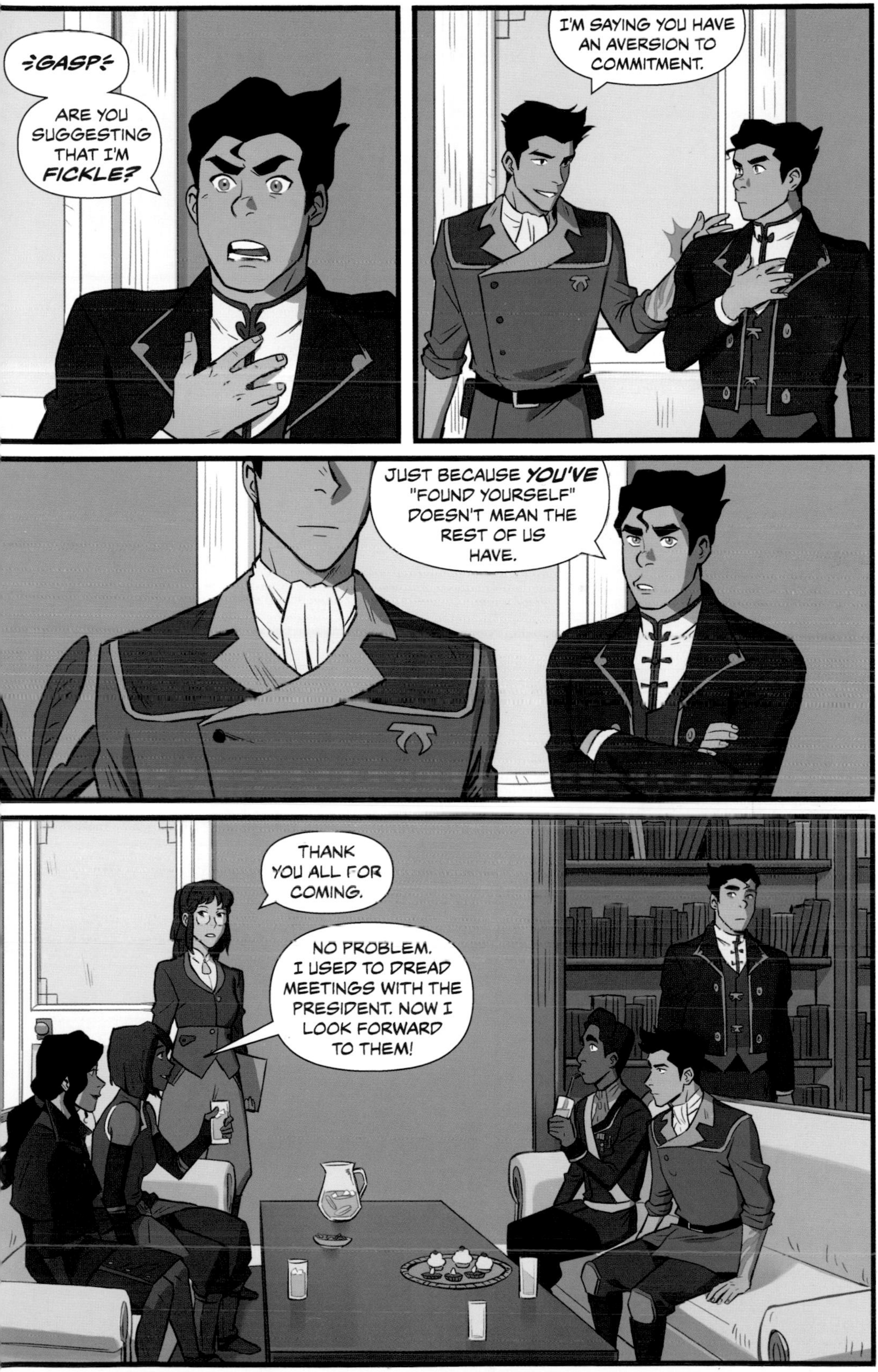

GASP
ARE YOU SUGGESTING THAT I'M FICKLE?
I'M SAYING YOU HAVE AN AVERSION TO COMMITMENT.
JUST BECAUSE YOU'VE "FOUND YOURSELF" DOESN'T MEAN THE REST OF US HAVE.
THANK YOU ALL FOR COMING.
NO PROBLEM. I USED TO DREAD MEETINGS WITH THE PRESIDENT. NOW I LOOK FORWARD TO THEM!

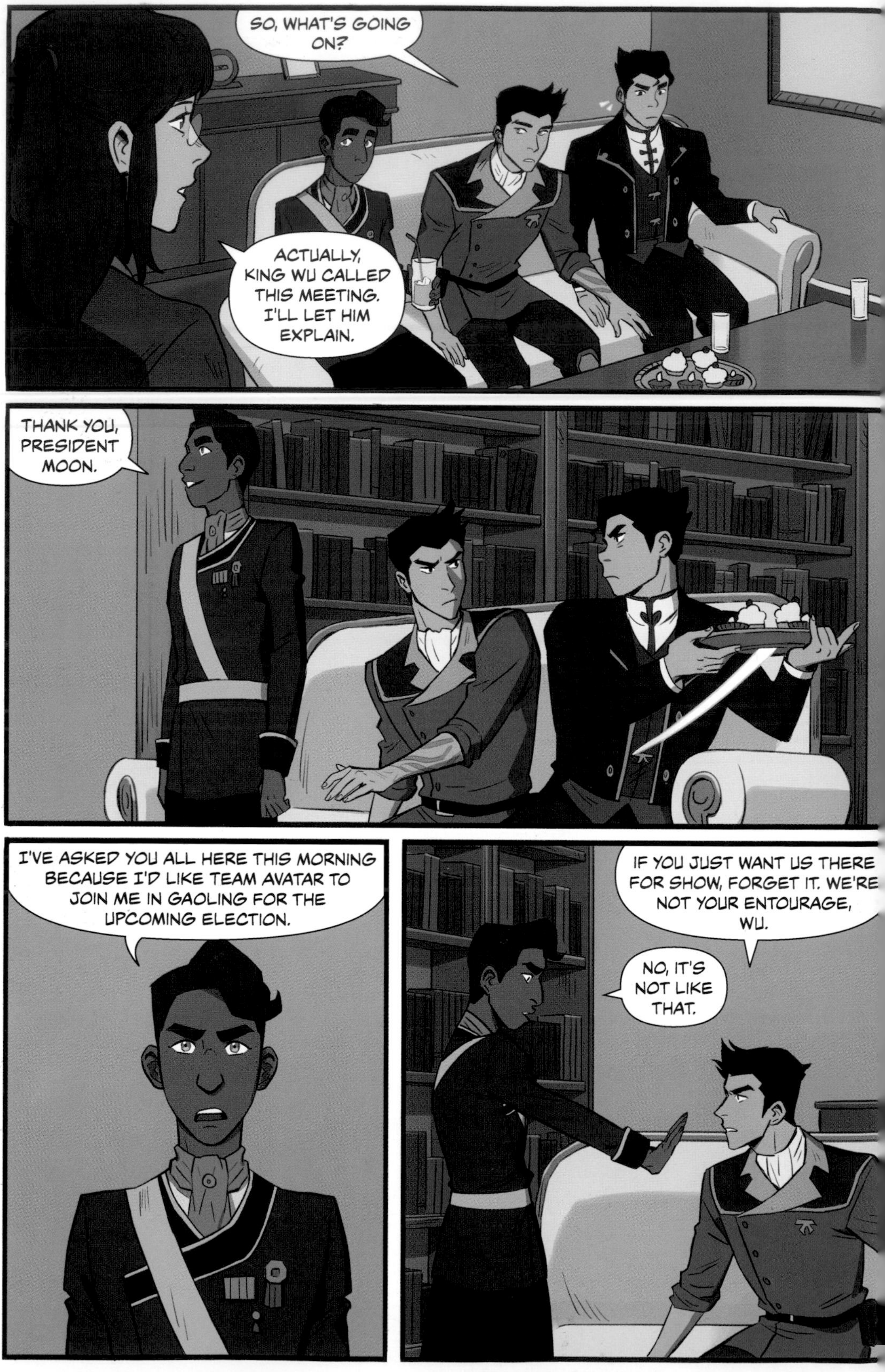

SO, WHAT'S GOING ON?
ACTUALLY, KING WU CALLED THIS MEETING. I'LL LET HIM EXPLAIN.
THANK YOU, PRESIDENT MOON.
I'VE ASKED YOU ALL HERE THIS MORNING BECAUSE I'D LIKE TEAM AVATAR TO JOIN ME IN GAOLING FOR THE UPCOMING ELECTION.
IF YOU JUST WANT US THERE FOR SHOW, FORGET IT. WE'RE NOT YOUR ENTOURAGE, WU.
NO, IT'S NOT LIKE THAT.

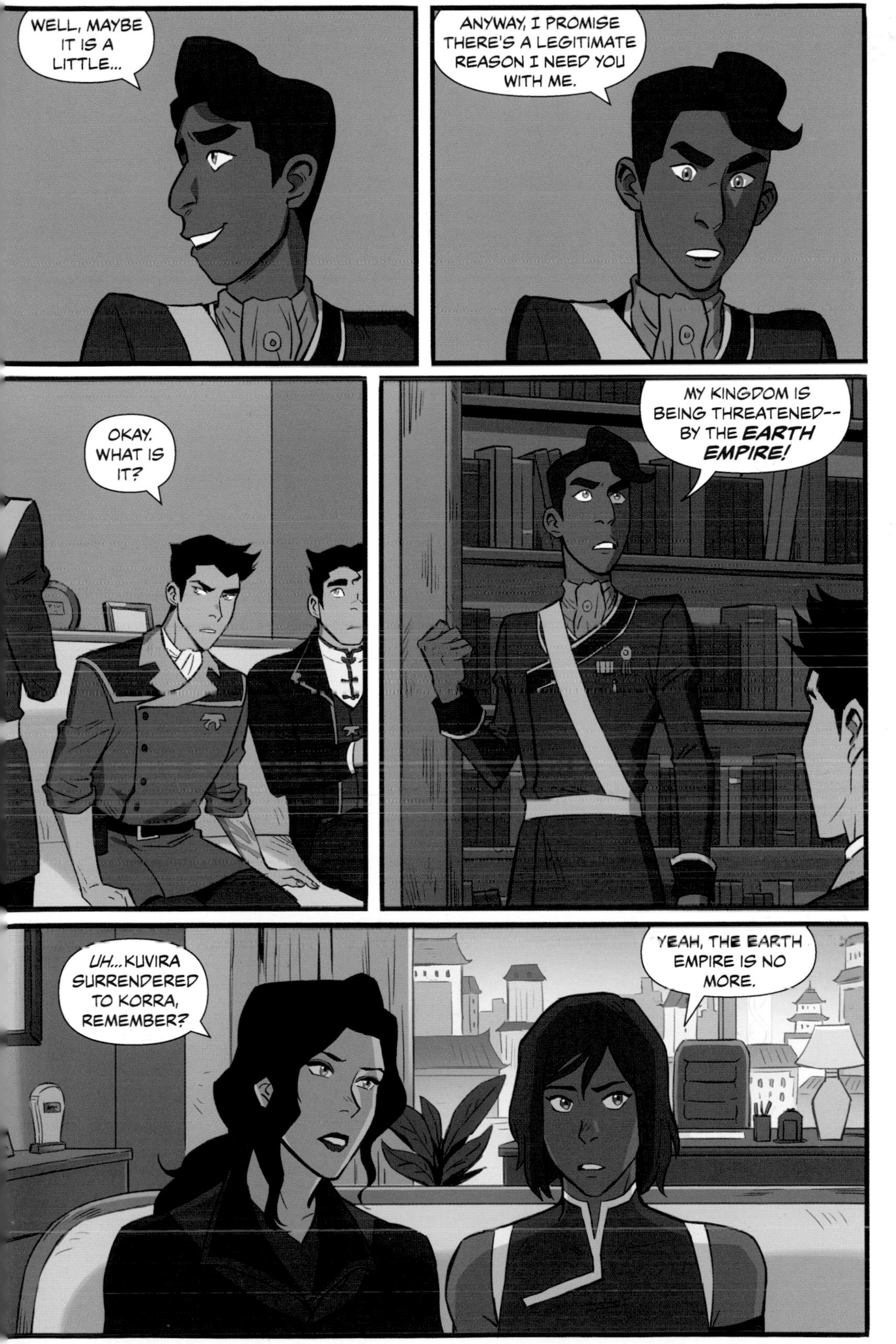
WELL, MAYBE IT IS A LITTLE...
ANYWAY, I PROMISE THERE'S A LEGITIMATE REASON I NEED YOU WITH ME.
OKAY. WHAT IS IT?
MY KINGDOM IS BEING THREATENED-- BY THE EARTH EMPIRE!
UH...KUVIRA SURRENDERED TO KORRA, REMEMBER?
YEAH, THE EARTH EMPIRE IS NO MORE.

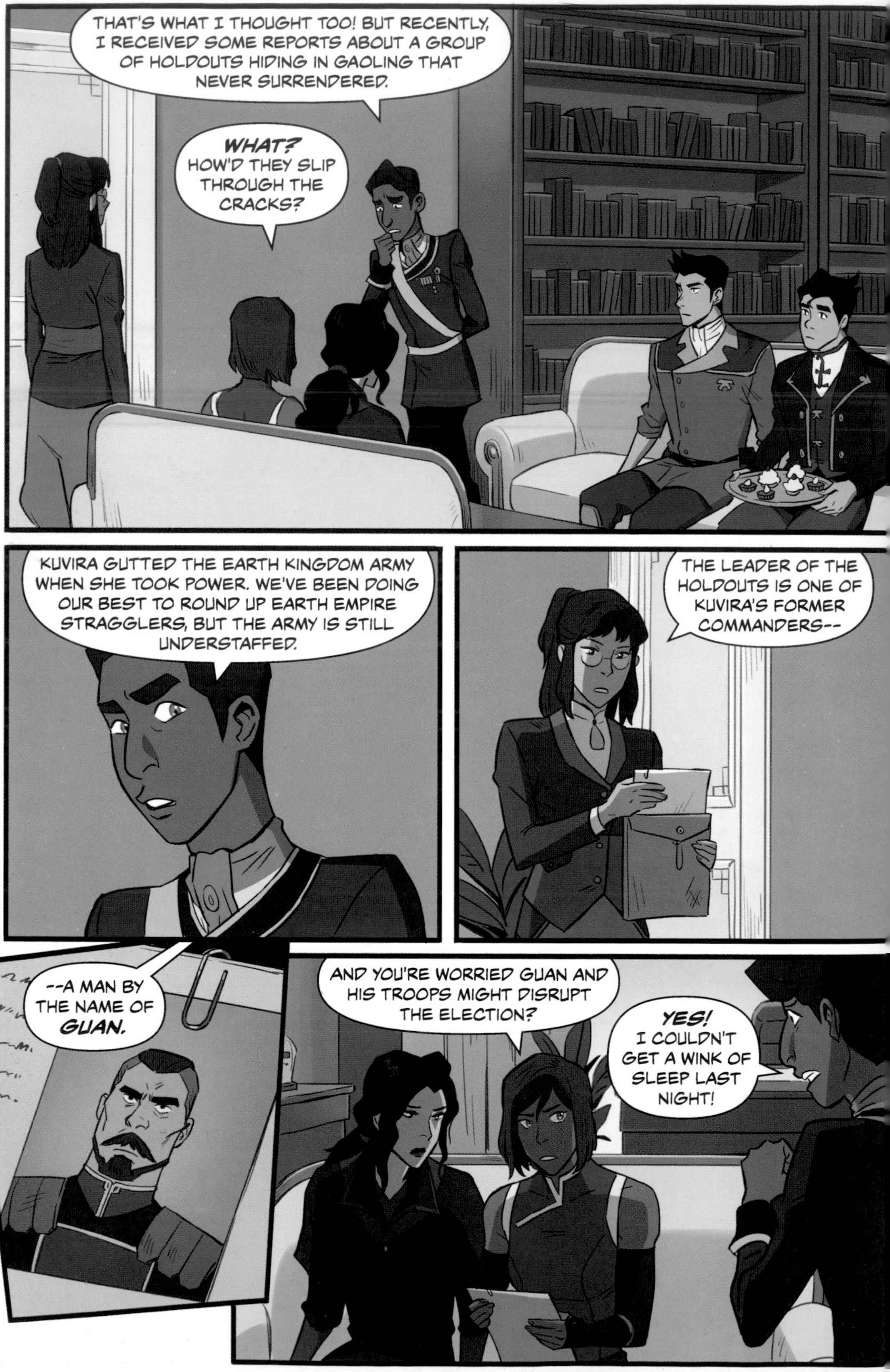
THAT'S WHAT I THOUGHT TOO! BUT RECENTLY, I RECEIVED SOME REPORTS ABOUT A GROUP OF HOLDOUTS HIDING IN GAOLING THAT NEVER SURRENDERED.
WHAT? HOW'D THEY SLIP THROUGH THE CRACKS?
KUVIRA GUTTED THE EARTH KINGDOM ARMY WHEN SHE TOOK POWER. WE'VE BEEN DOING OUR BEST TO ROUND UP EARTH EMPIRE STRAGGLERS, BUT THE ARMY IS STILL UNDERSTAFFED.
THE LEADER OF THE HOLDOUTS IS ONE OF KUVIRA'S FORMER COMMANDERS--
--A MAN BY THE NAME OF GUAN.
AND YOU'RE WORRIED GUAN AND HIS TROOPS MIGHT DISRUPT THE ELECTION?
YES! I COULDN'T GET A WINK OF SLEEP LAST NIGHT!

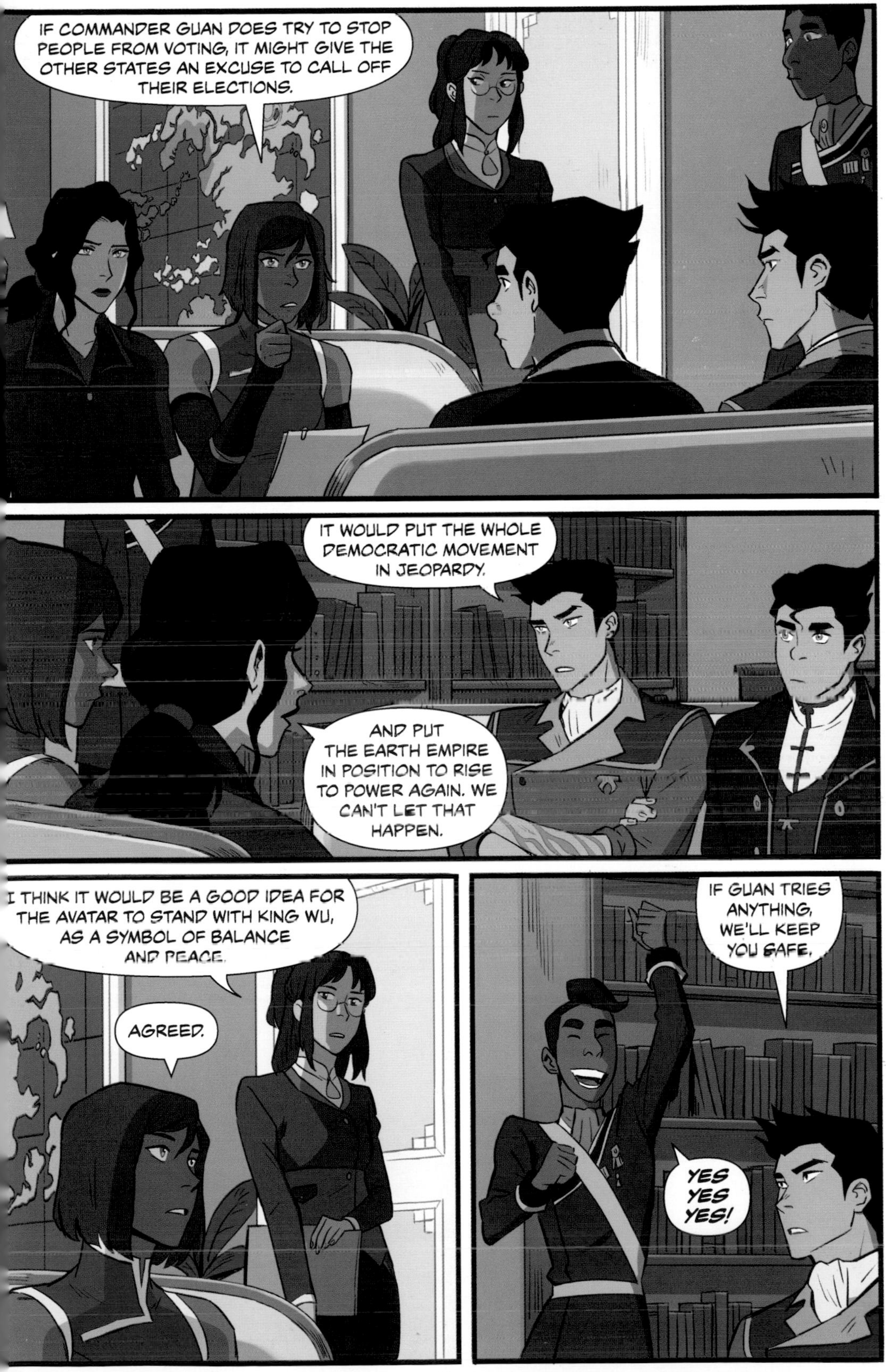
IF COMMANDER GUAN DOES TRY TO STOP PEOPLE FROM VOTING, IT MIGHT GIVE THE OTHER STATES AN EXCUSE TO CALL OFF THEIR ELECTIONS.
IT WOULD PUT THE WHOLE DEMOCRATIC MOVEMENT IN JEOPARDY.
AND PUT THE EARTH EMPIRE IN POSITION TO RISE TO POWER AGAIN. WE CAN'T LET THAT HAPPEN.
I THINK IT WOULD BE A GOOD IDEA FOR THE AVATAR TO STAND WITH KING WU, AS A SYMBOL OF BALANCE AND PEACE.
AGREED.
IF GUAN TRIES ANYTHING, WE'LL KEEP YOU SAFE.
YES YES YES!

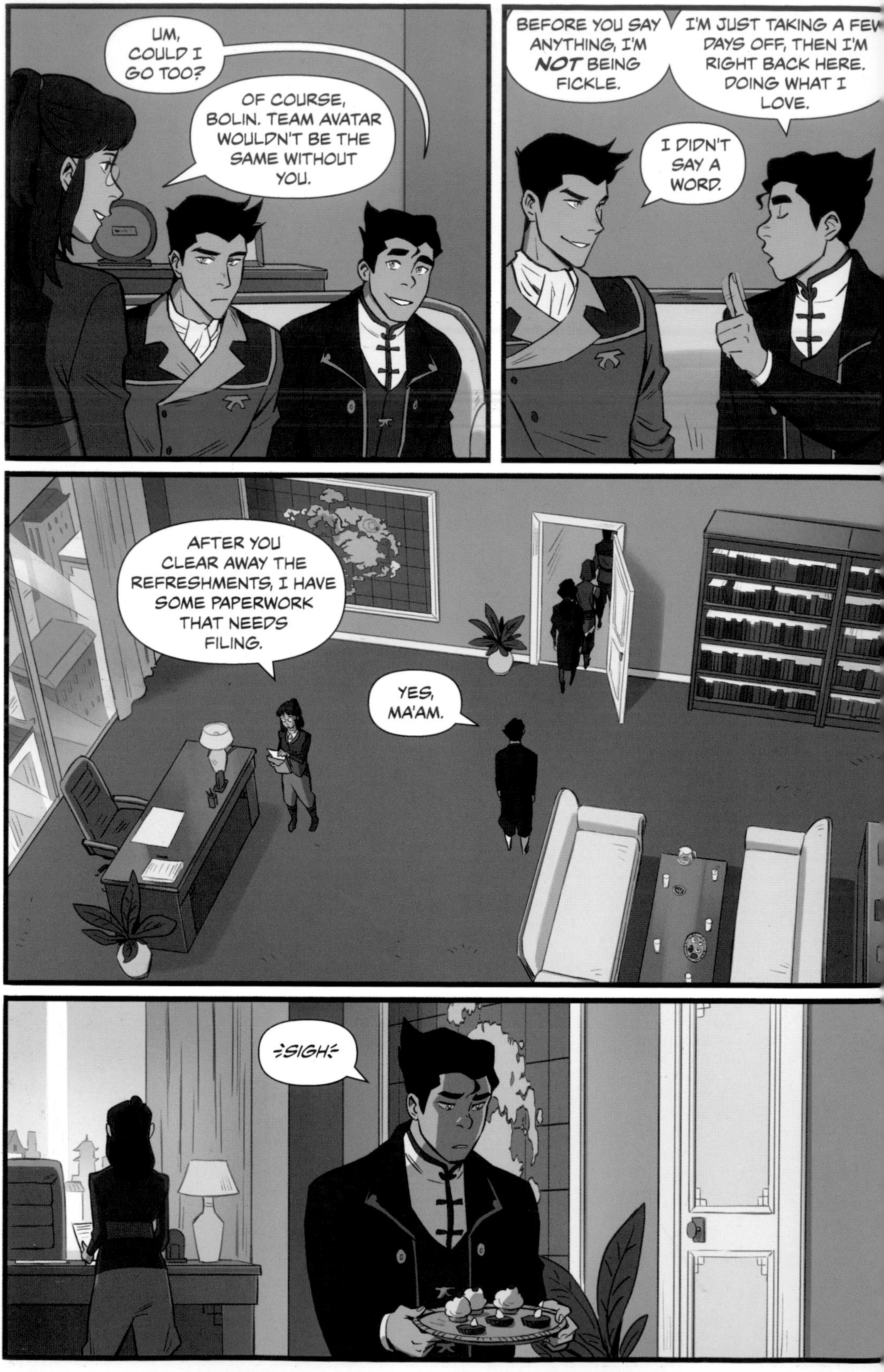
UM, COULD I GO TOO?
OF COURSE, BOLIN. TEAM AVATAR WOULDN'T BE THE SAME WITHOUT YOU.
BEFORE YOU SAY ANYTHING, I'M *NOT* BEING FICKLE.
I'M JUST TAKING A FEW DAYS OFF, THEN I'M RIGHT BACK HERE. DOING WHAT I LOVE.
I DIDN'T SAY A WORD.
AFTER YOU CLEAR AWAY THE REFRESHMENTS, I HAVE SOME PAPERWORK THAT NEEDS FILING.
YES, MA'AM.
SIGH

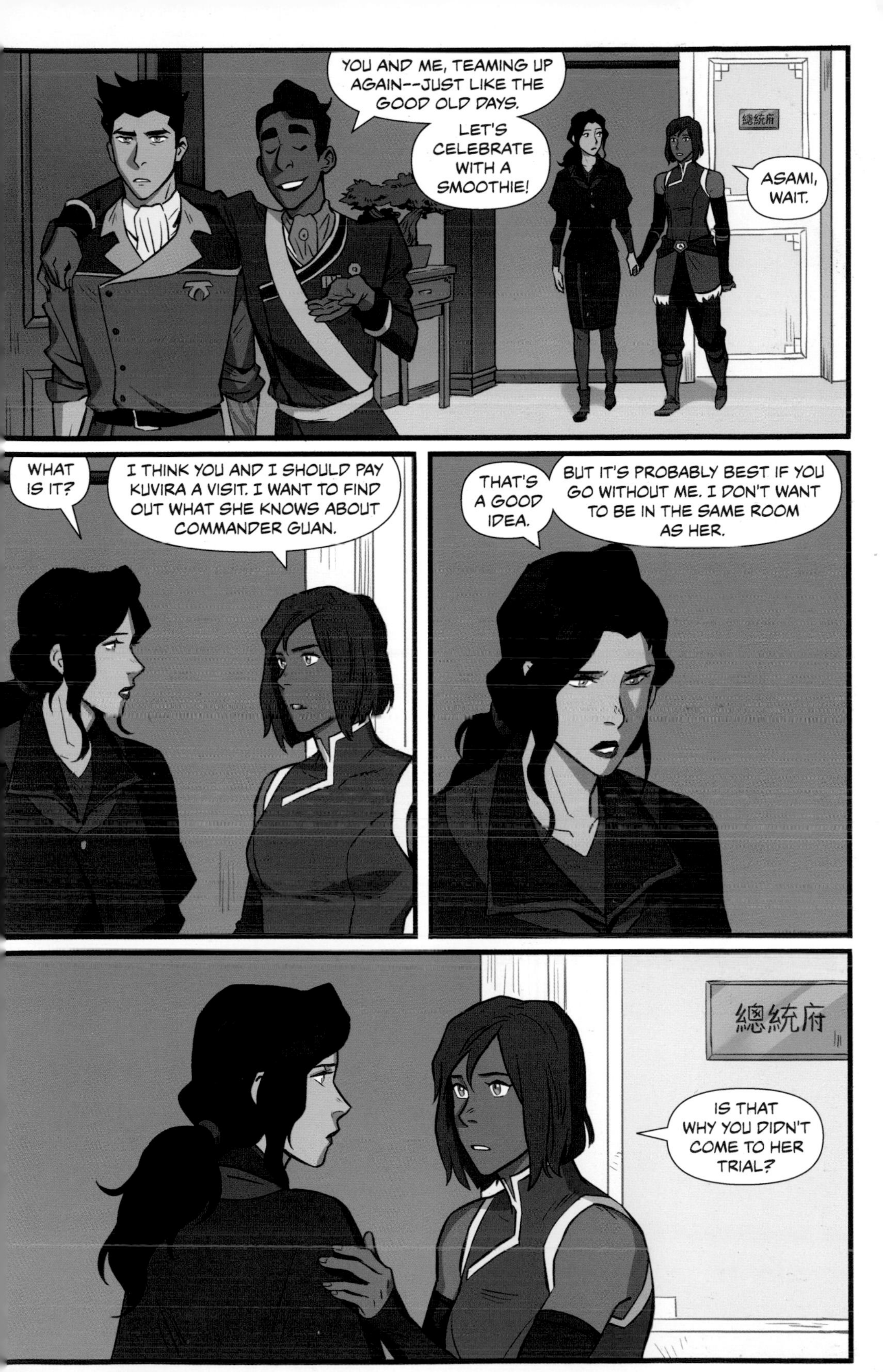
YOU AND ME, TEAMING UP AGAIN--JUST LIKE THE GOOD OLD DAYS.
LET'S CELEBRATE WITH A SMOOTHIE!
總統府
ASAMI, WAIT.
WHAT IS IT?
I THINK YOU AND I SHOULD PAY KUVIRA A VISIT. I WANT TO FIND OUT WHAT SHE KNOWS ABOUT COMMANDER GUAN.
THAT'S A GOOD IDEA.
BUT IT'S PROBABLY BEST IF YOU GO WITHOUT ME. I DON'T WANT TO BE IN THE SAME ROOM AS HER.
總統府
IS THAT WHY YOU DIDN'T COME TO HER TRIAL?

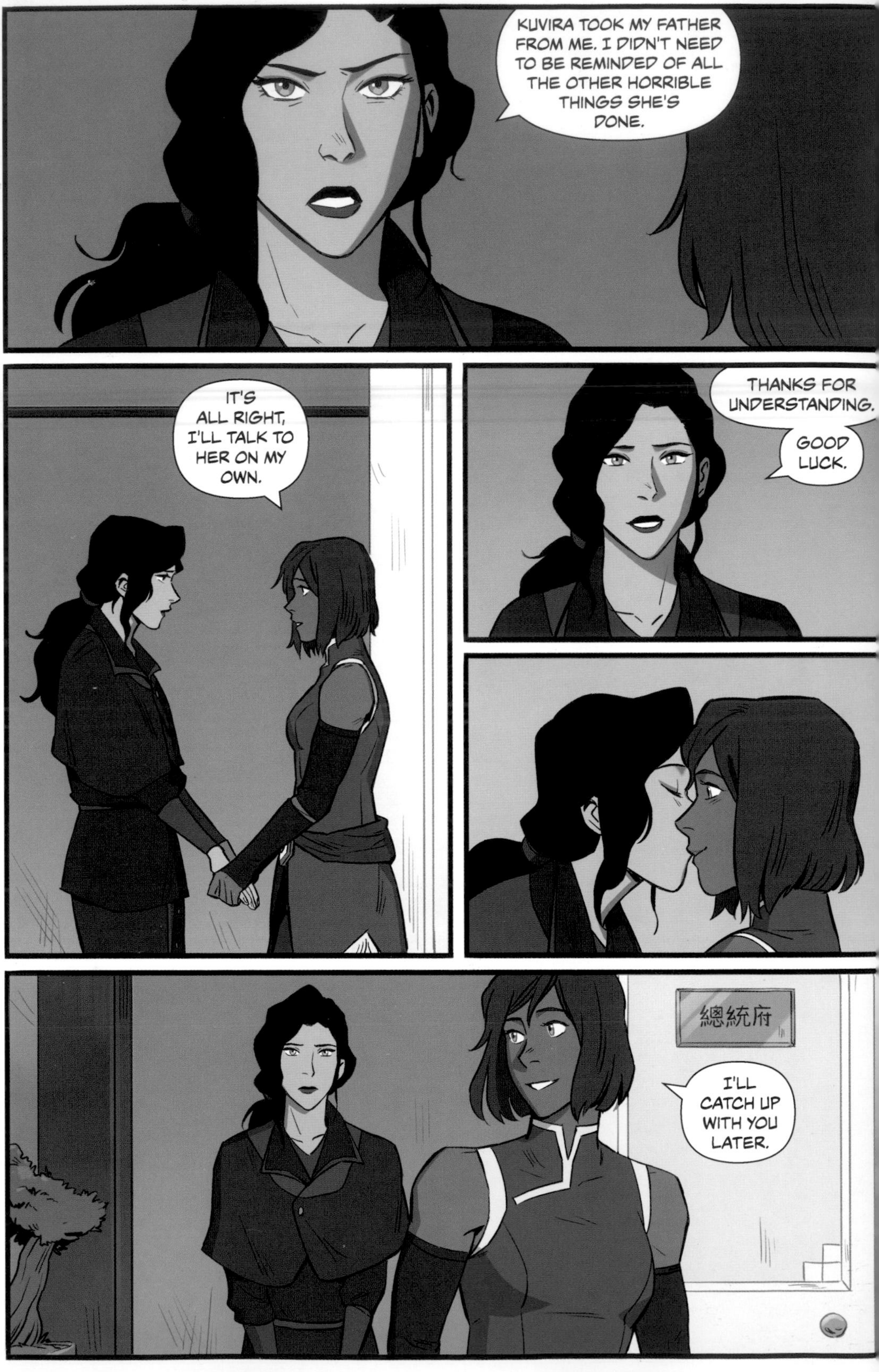
KUVIRA TOOK MY FATHER FROM ME. I DIDN'T NEED TO BE REMINDED OF ALL THE OTHER HORRIBLE THINGS SHE'S DONE.
IT'S ALL RIGHT, I'LL TALK TO HER ON MY OWN.
THANKS FOR UNDERSTANDING.
GOOD LUCK.
總統府
I'LL CATCH UP WITH YOU LATER.

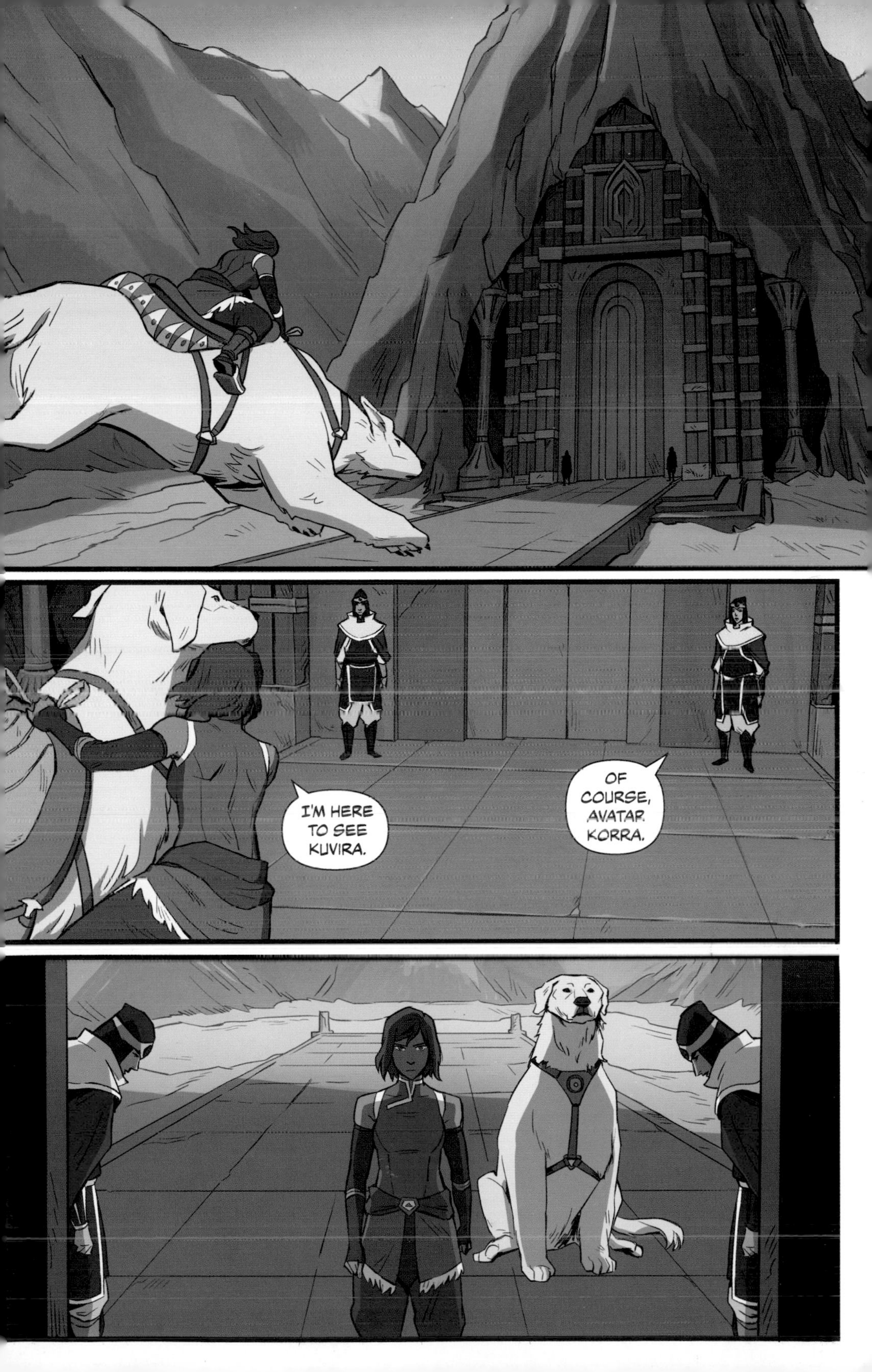
I'M HERE TO SEE KUVIRA.
OF COURSE, AVATAR KORRA.

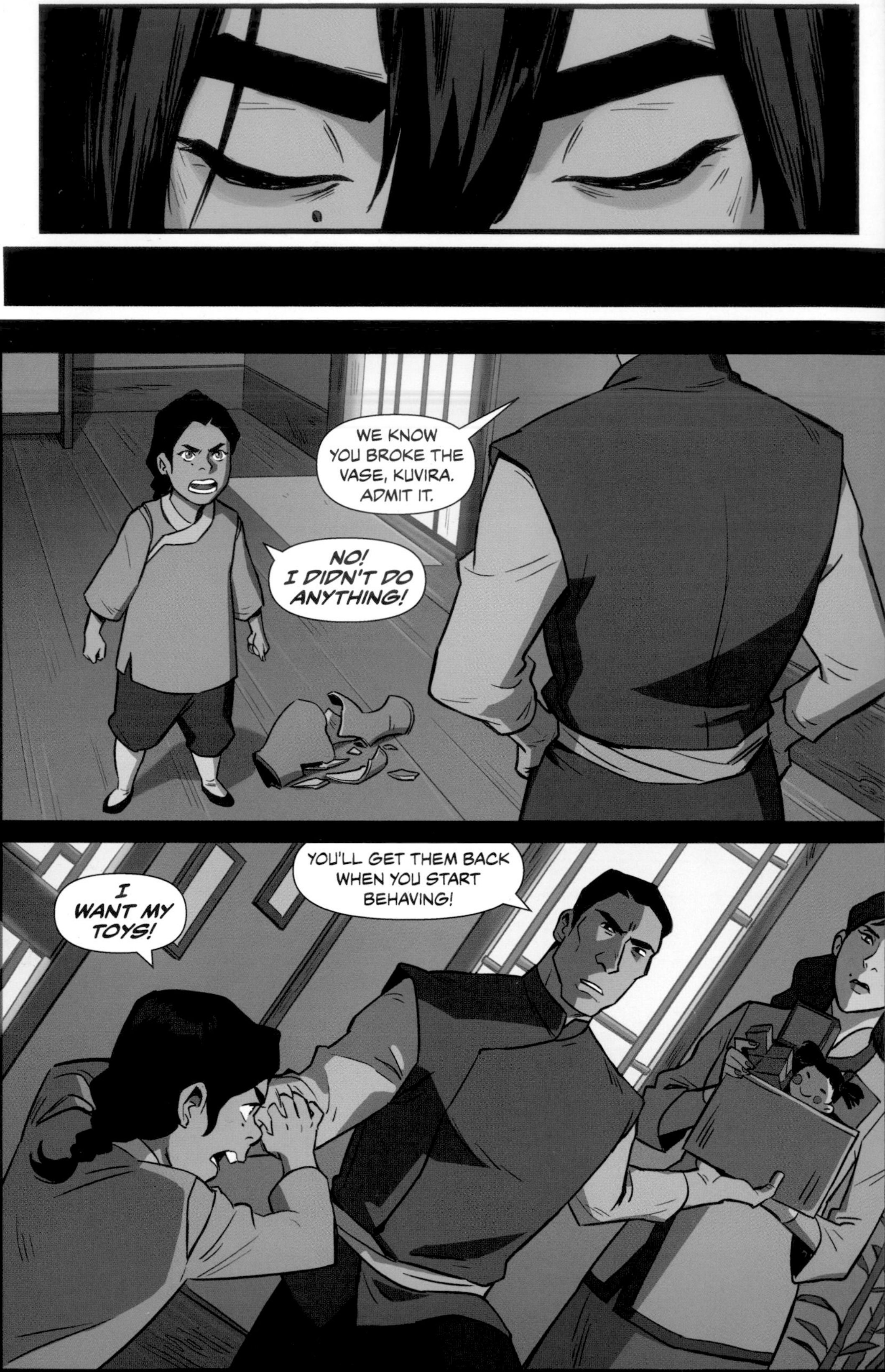
WE KNOW YOU BROKE THE VASE, KUVIRA. ADMIT IT.
NO! I DIDN'T DO ANYTHING!
I WANT MY TOYS!
YOU'LL GET THEM BACK WHEN YOU START BEHAVING!

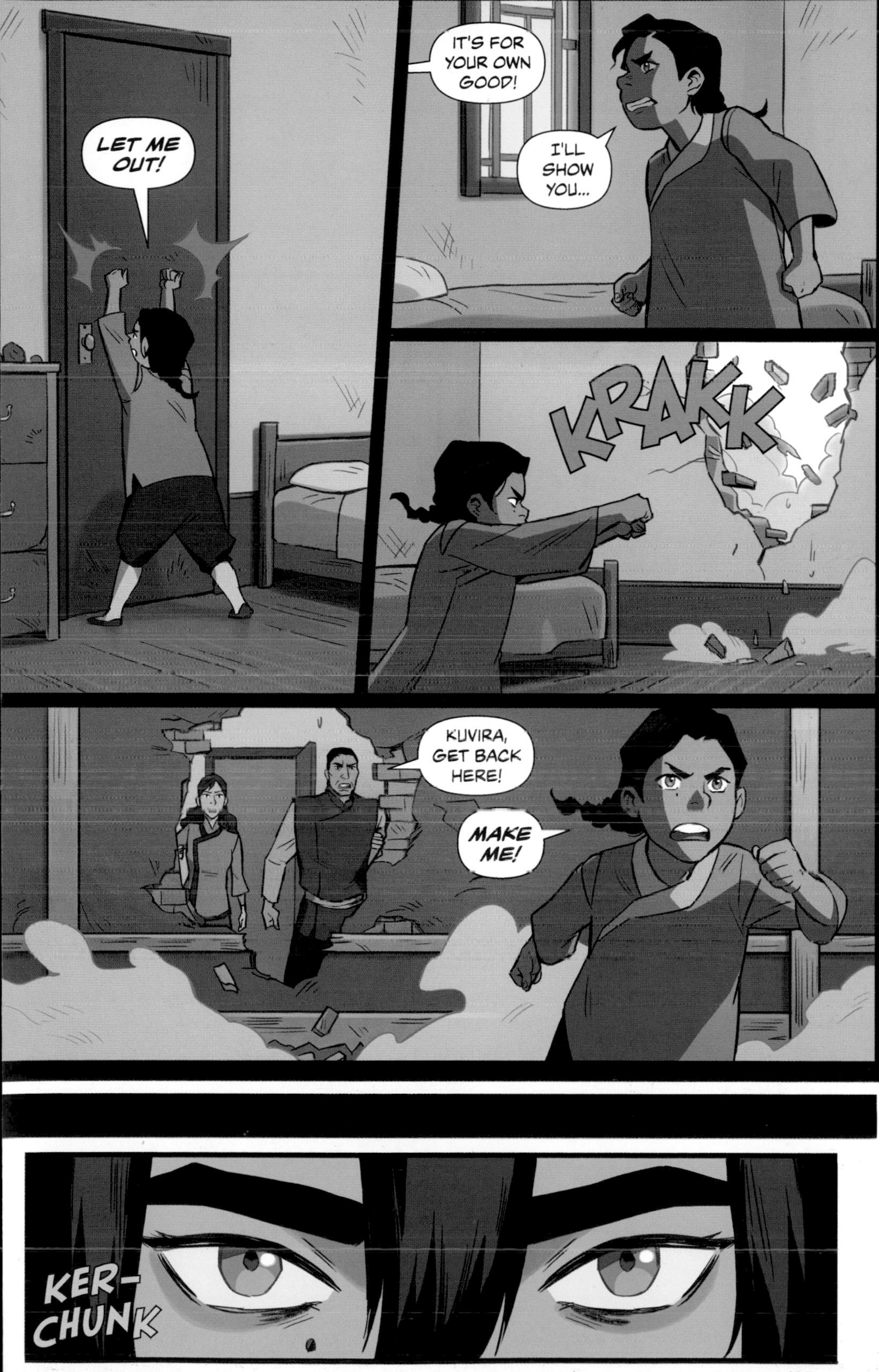
LET ME OUT!
IT'S FOR YOUR OWN GOOD!
I'LL SHOW YOU...
KRAKK
KUVIRA, GET BACK HERE!
MAKE ME!
KER-CHUNK

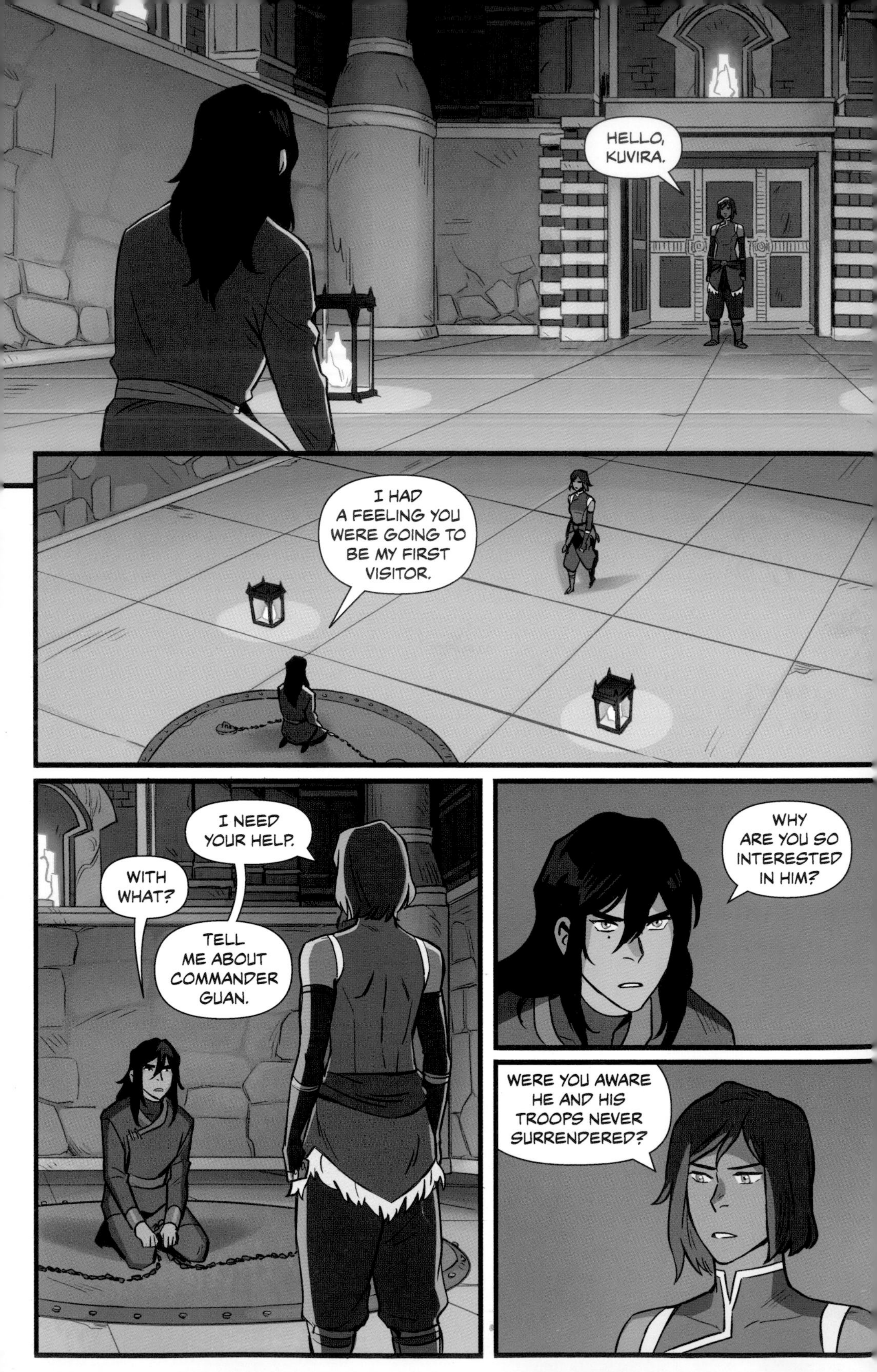
HELLO, KUVIRA.
I HAD A FEELING YOU WERE GOING TO BE MY FIRST VISITOR.
I NEED YOUR HELP.
WITH WHAT?
TELL ME ABOUT COMMANDER GUAN.
WHY ARE YOU SO INTERESTED IN HIM?
WERE YOU AWARE HE AND HIS TROOPS NEVER SURRENDERED?

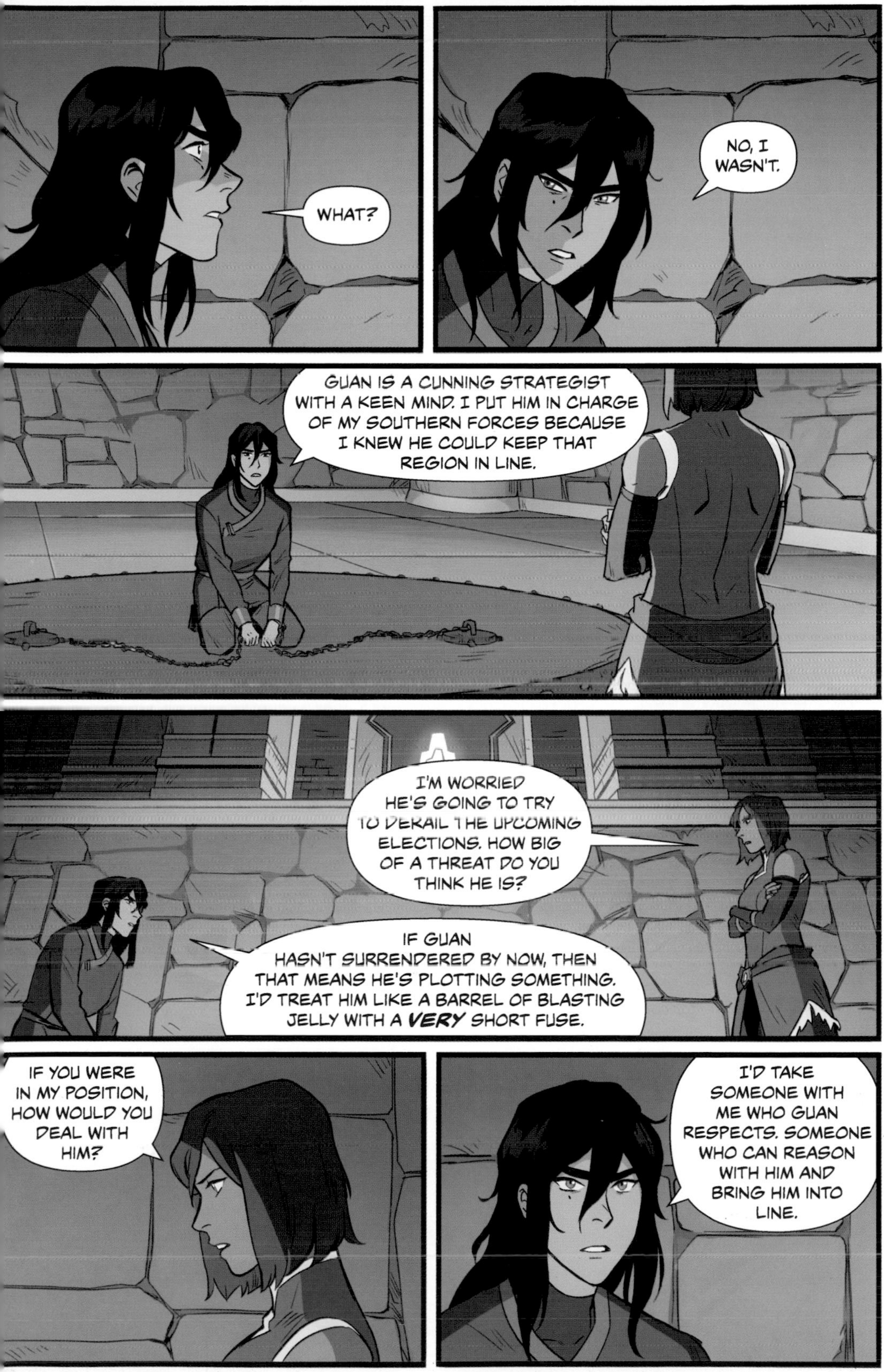
WHAT?
NO, I WASN'T.
GUAN IS A CUNNING STRATEGIST WITH A KEEN MIND. I PUT HIM IN CHARGE OF MY SOUTHERN FORCES BECAUSE I KNEW HE COULD KEEP THAT REGION IN LINE.
I'M WORRIED HE'S GOING TO TRY TO DERAIL THE UPCOMING ELECTIONS. HOW BIG OF A THREAT DO YOU THINK HE IS?
IF GUAN HASN'T SURRENDERED BY NOW, THEN THAT MEANS HE'S PLOTTING SOMETHING. I'D TREAT HIM LIKE A BARREL OF BLASTING JELLY WITH A *VERY* SHORT FUSE.
IF YOU WERE IN MY POSITION, HOW WOULD YOU DEAL WITH HIM?
I'D TAKE SOMEONE WITH ME WHO GUAN RESPECTS. SOMEONE WHO CAN REASON WITH HIM AND BRING HIM INTO LINE.

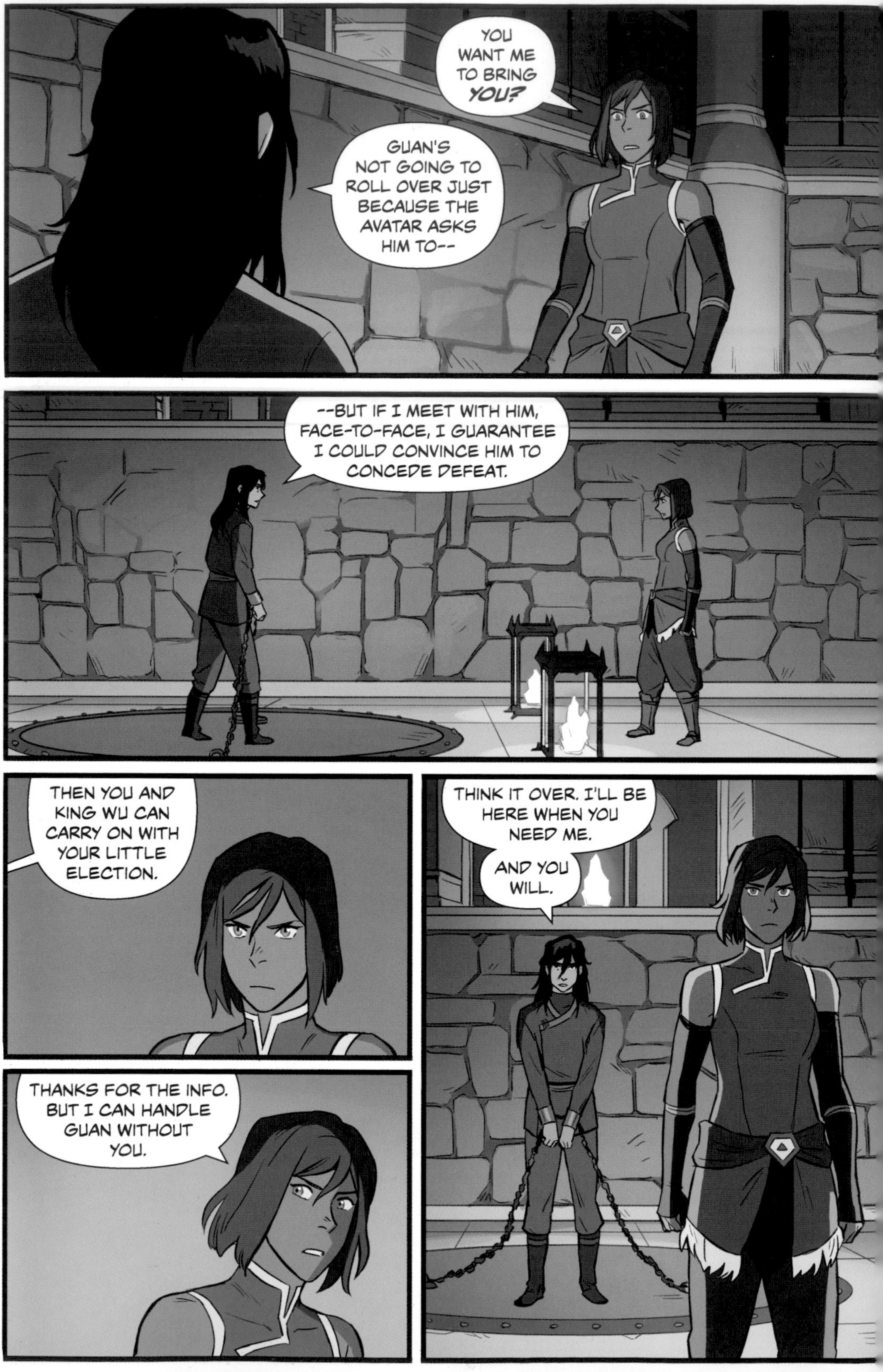
YOU WANT ME TO BRING *YOU?*
GUAN'S NOT GOING TO ROLL OVER JUST BECAUSE THE AVATAR ASKS HIM TO--
--BUT IF I MEET WITH HIM, FACE-TO-FACE, I GUARANTEE I COULD CONVINCE HIM TO CONCEDE DEFEAT.
THEN YOU AND KING WU CAN CARRY ON WITH YOUR LITTLE ELECTION.
THANKS FOR THE INFO. BUT I CAN HANDLE GUAN WITHOUT YOU.
THINK IT OVER. I'LL BE HERE WHEN YOU NEED ME.
AND YOU WILL.

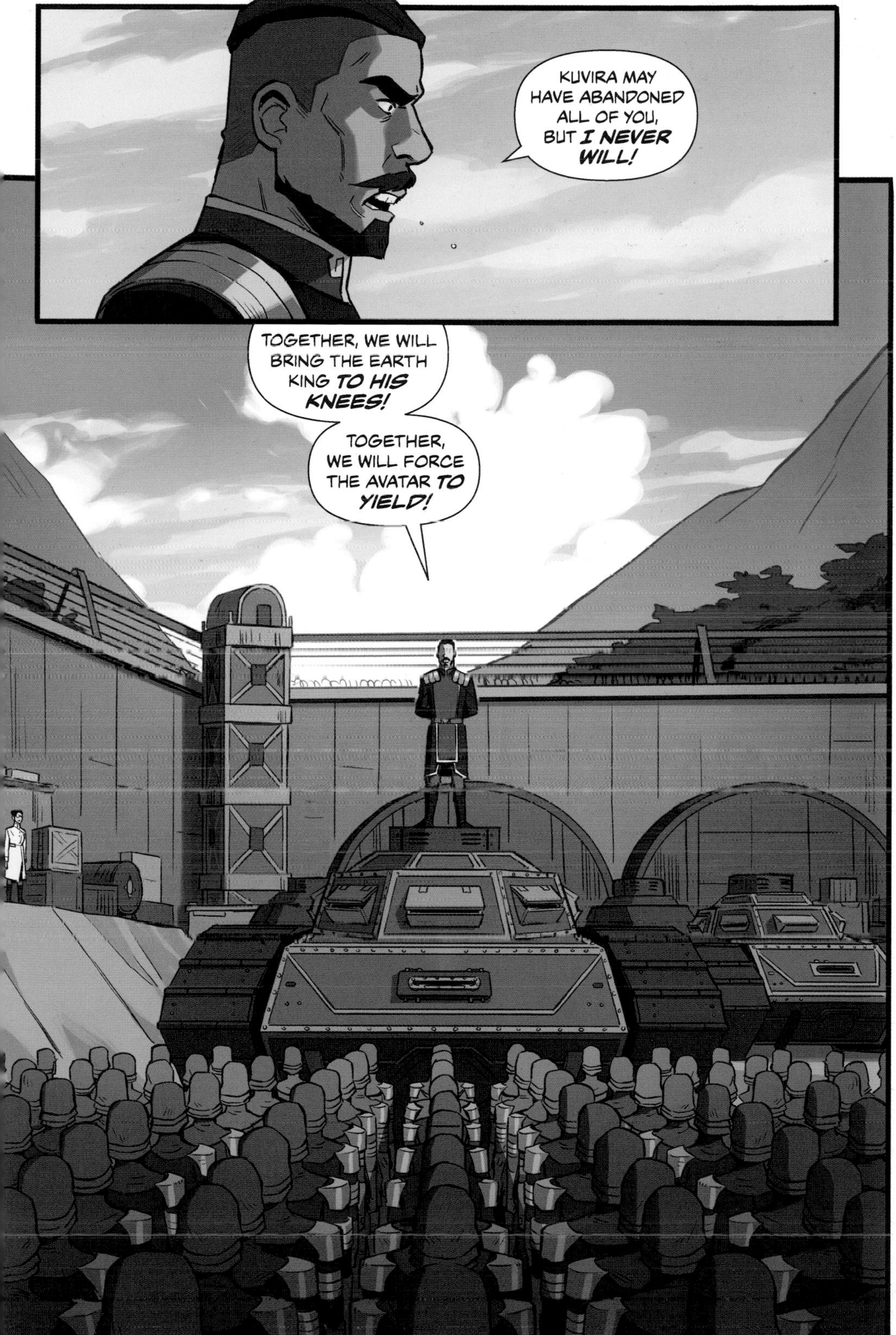
KUVIRA MAY HAVE ABANDONED ALL OF YOU, BUT I NEVER WILL!
TOGETHER, WE WILL BRING THE EARTH KING TO HIS KNEES!
TOGETHER, WE WILL FORCE THE AVATAR TO YIELD!

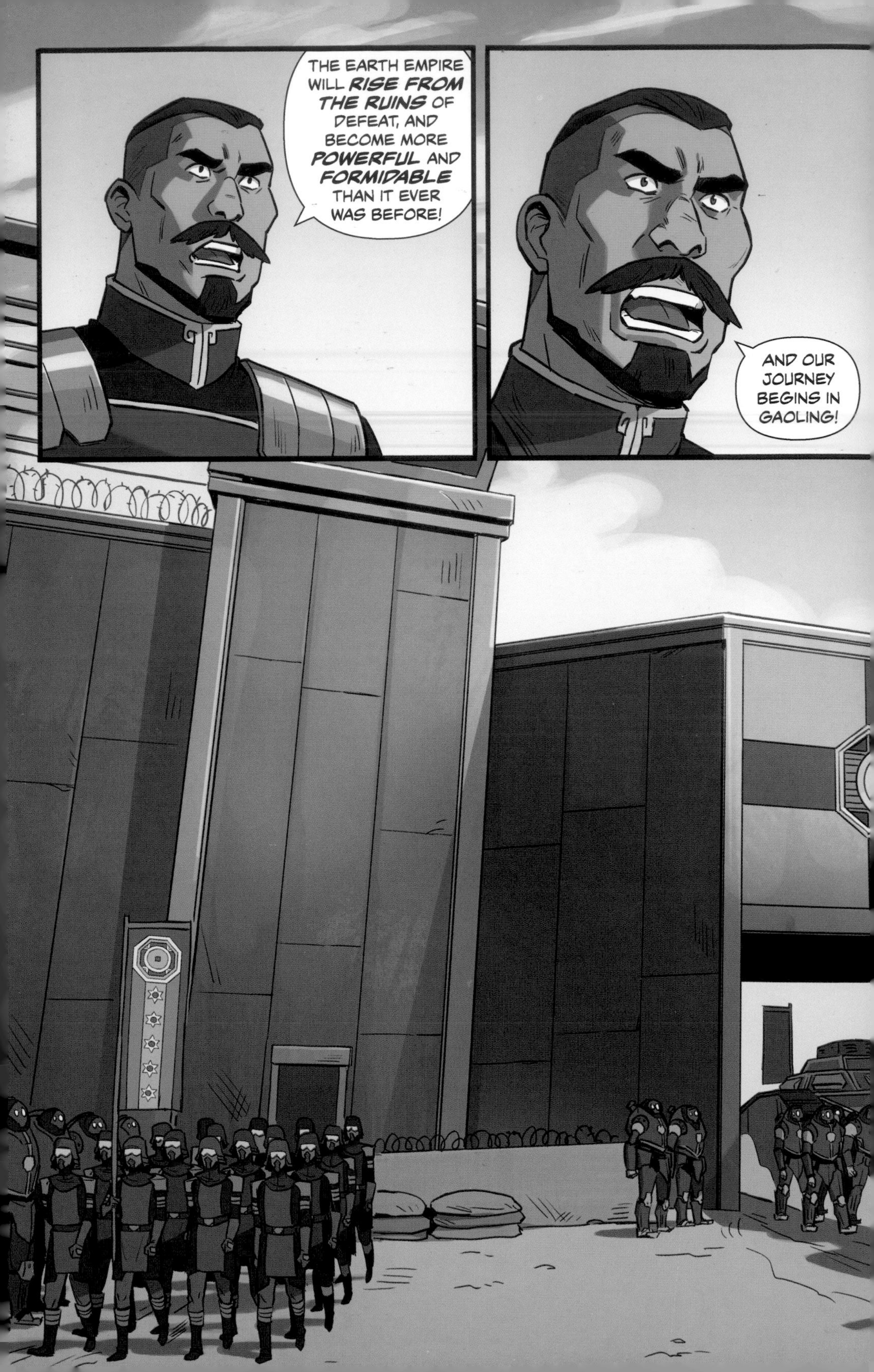
THE EARTH EMPIRE WILL RISE FROM THE RUINS OF DEFEAT, AND BECOME MORE POWERFUL AND FORMIDABLE THAN IT EVER WAS BEFORE!
AND OUR JOURNEY BEGINS IN GAOLING!

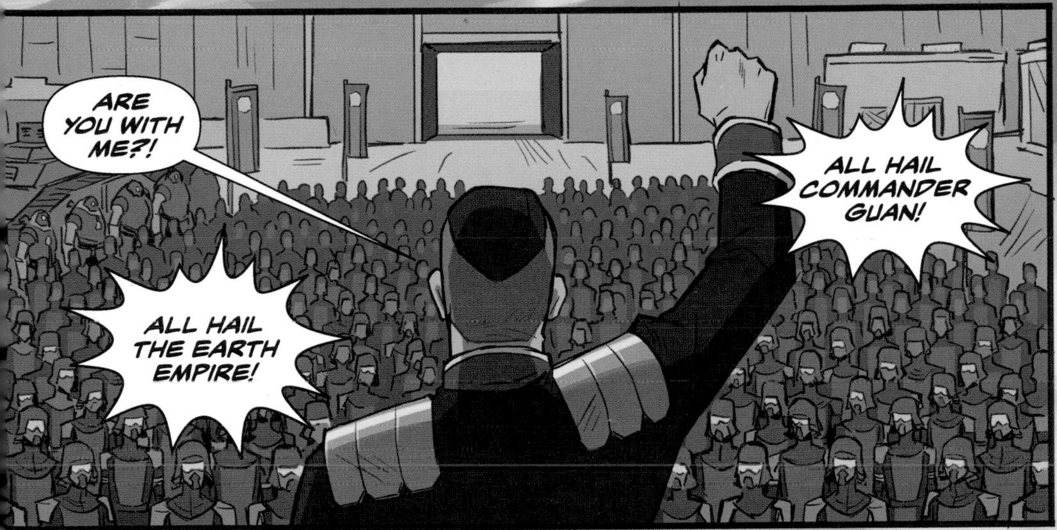
ARE YOU WITH ME?!
ALL HAIL COMMANDER GUAN!
ALL HAIL THE EARTH EMPIRE!

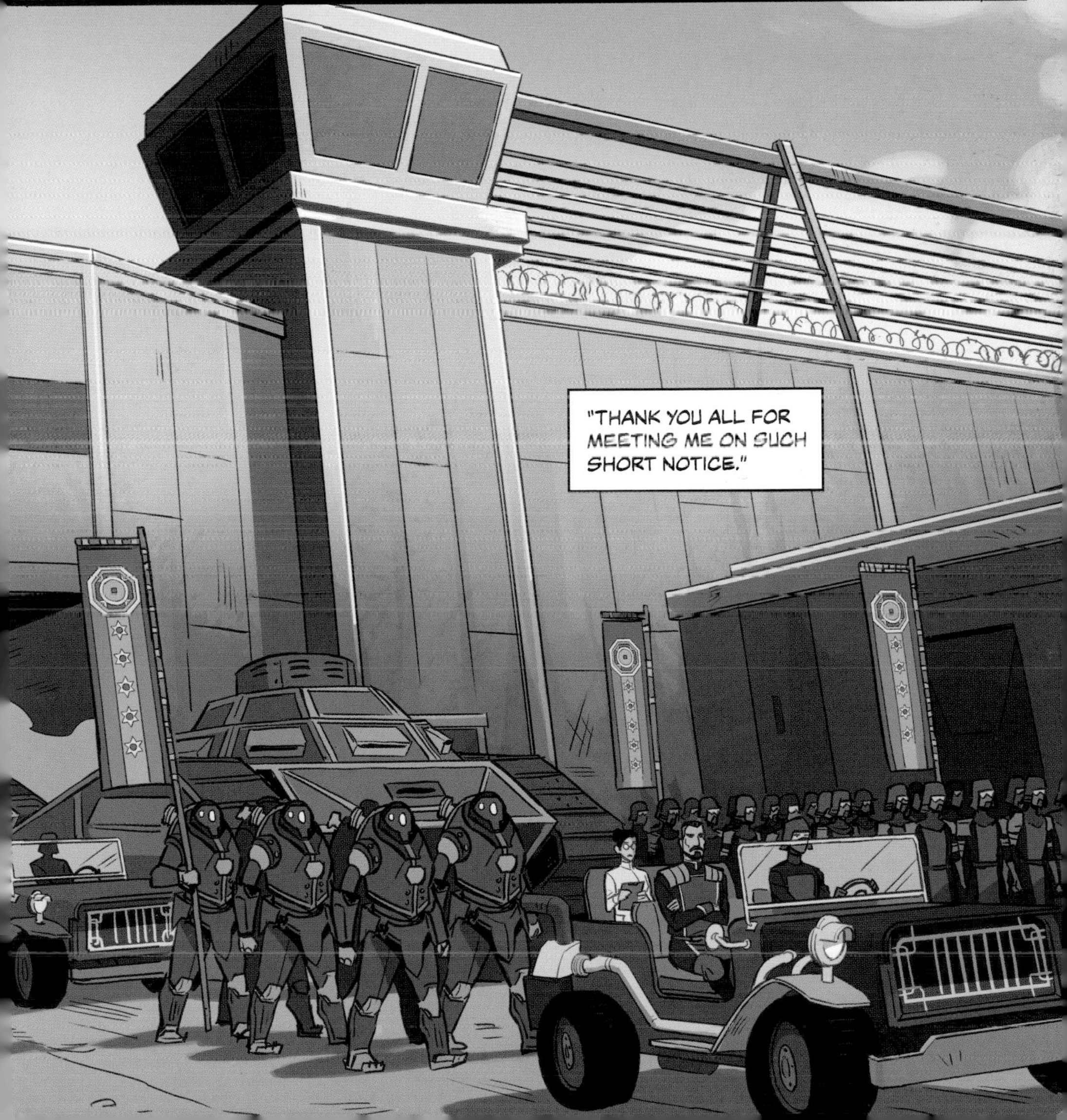
"THANK YOU ALL FOR MEETING ME ON SUCH SHORT NOTICE."

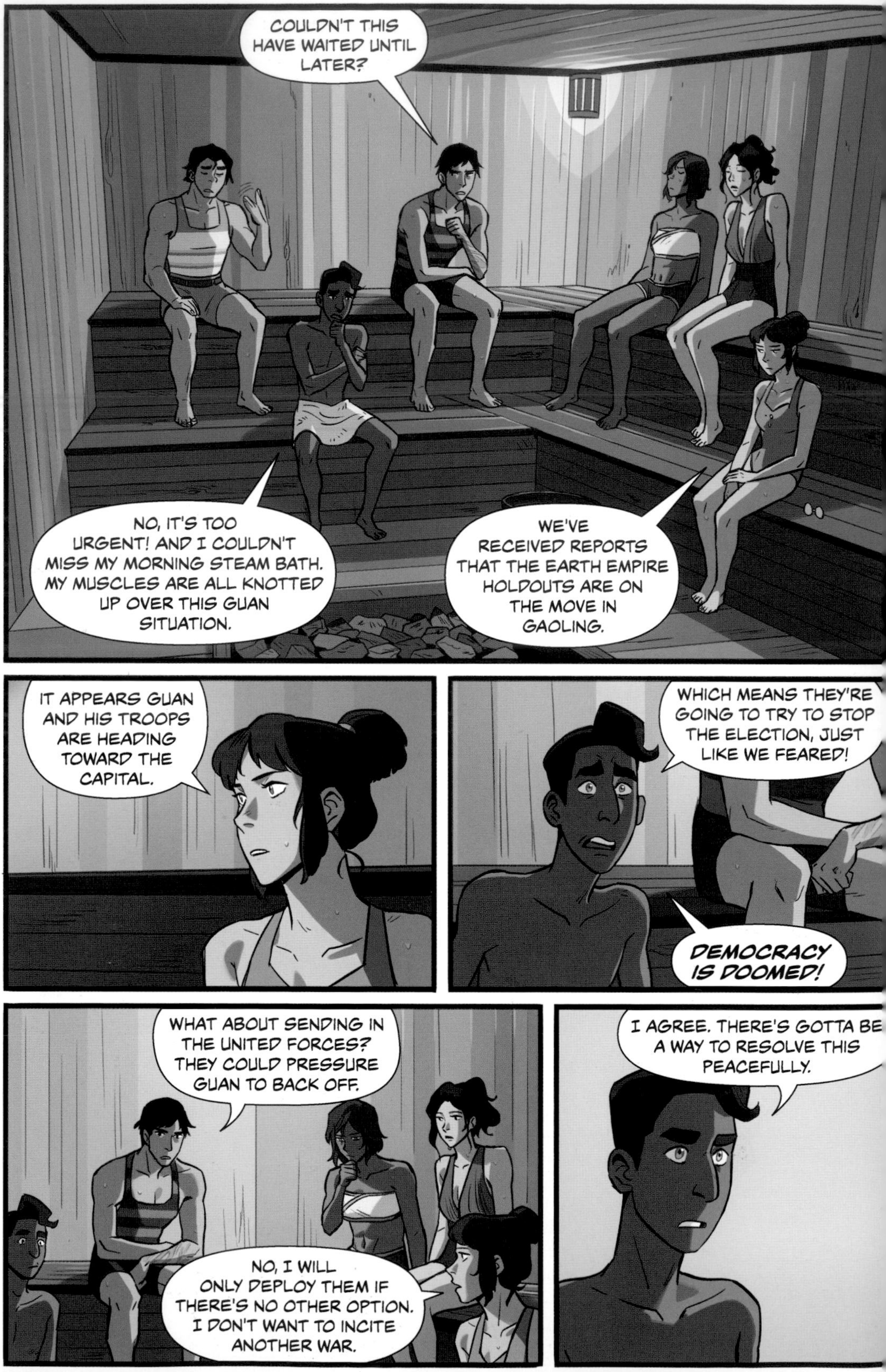
COULDN'T THIS HAVE WAITED UNTIL LATER?
NO, IT'S TOO URGENT! AND I COULDN'T MISS MY MORNING STEAM BATH. MY MUSCLES ARE ALL KNOTTED UP OVER THIS GUAN SITUATION.
WE'VE RECEIVED REPORTS THAT THE EARTH EMPIRE HOLDOUTS ARE ON THE MOVE IN GAOLING.
IT APPEARS GUAN AND HIS TROOPS ARE HEADING TOWARD THE CAPITAL.
WHICH MEANS THEY'RE GOING TO TRY TO STOP THE ELECTION, JUST LIKE WE FEARED!
DEMOCRACY IS DOOMED!
WHAT ABOUT SENDING IN THE UNITED FORCES? THEY COULD PRESSURE GUAN TO BACK OFF.
NO, I WILL ONLY DEPLOY THEM IF THERE'S NO OTHER OPTION. I DON'T WANT TO INCITE ANOTHER WAR.
I AGREE. THERE'S GOTTA BE A WAY TO RESOLVE THIS PEACEFULLY.

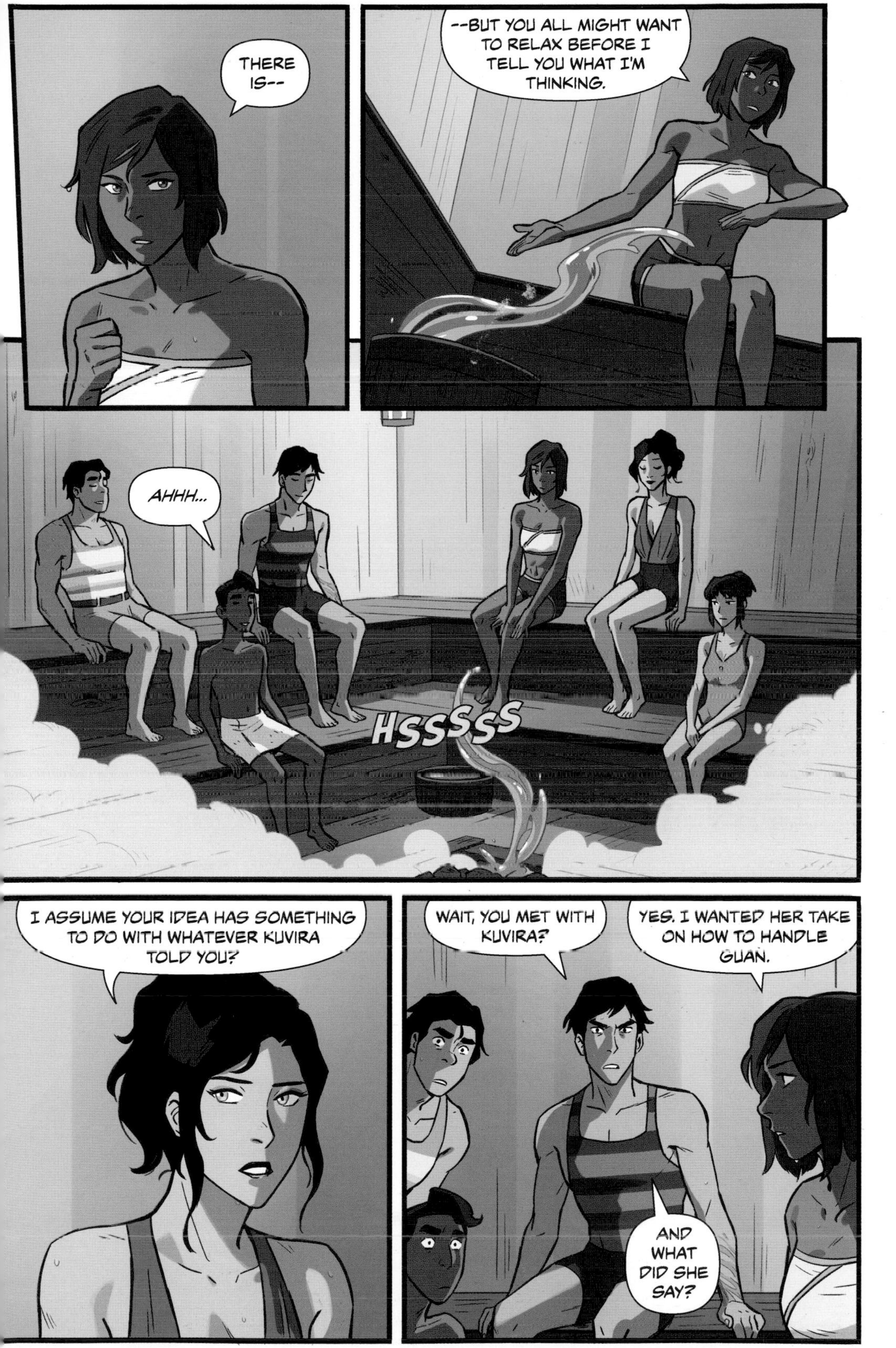
THERE IS--
--BUT YOU ALL MIGHT WANT TO RELAX BEFORE I TELL YOU WHAT I'M THINKING.
AHHH...
HSSSSS
I ASSUME YOUR IDEA HAS SOMETHING TO DO WITH WHATEVER KUVIRA TOLD YOU?
WAIT, YOU MET WITH KUVIRA?
YES. I WANTED HER TAKE ON HOW TO HANDLE GUAN.
AND WHAT DID SHE SAY?

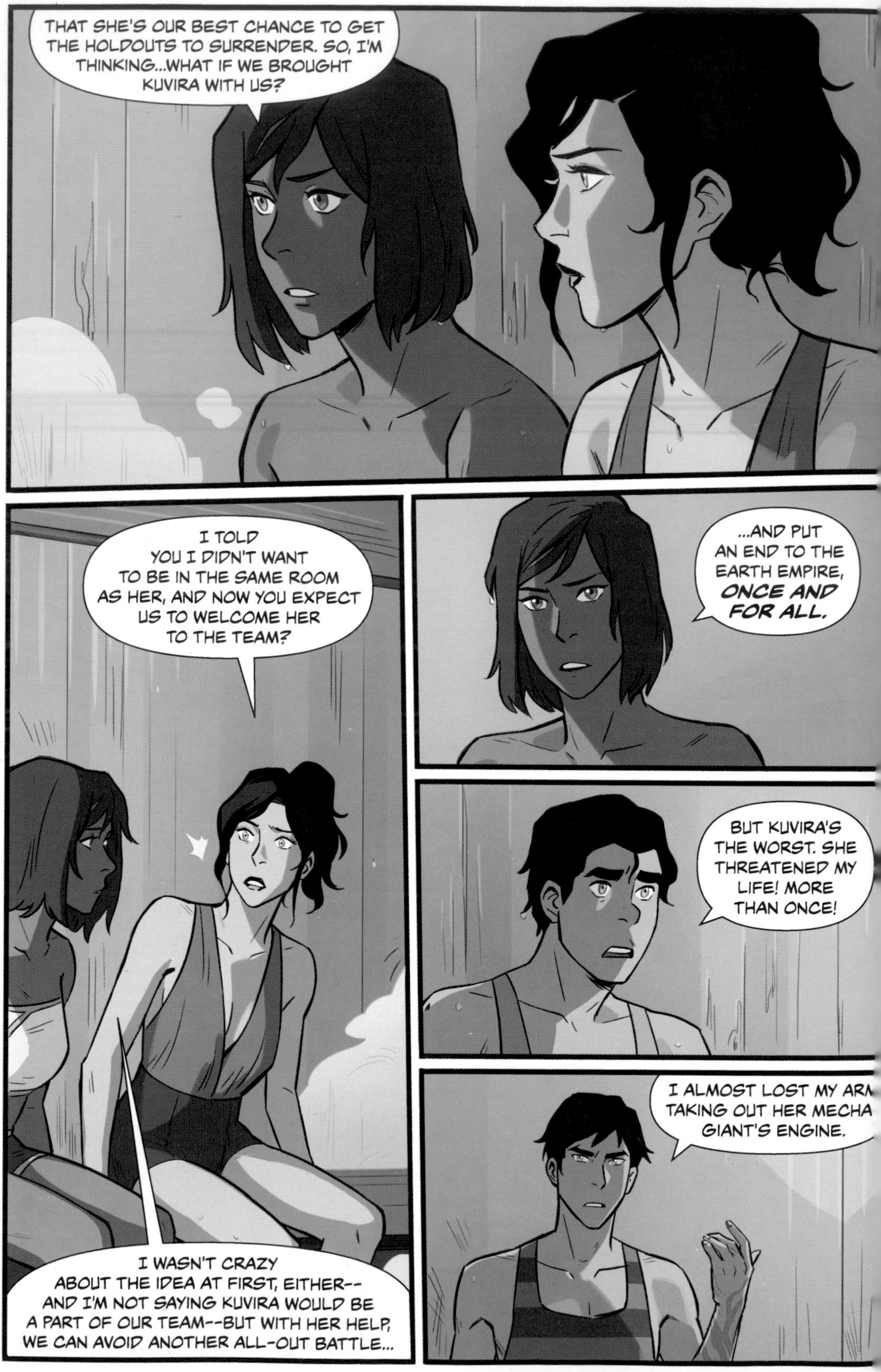

THAT SHE'S OUR BEST CHANCE TO GET THE HOLDOUTS TO SURRENDER. SO, I'M THINKING...WHAT IF WE BROUGHT KUVIRA WITH US?
I TOLD YOU I DIDN'T WANT TO BE IN THE SAME ROOM AS HER, AND NOW YOU EXPECT US TO WELCOME HER TO THE TEAM?
I WASN'T CRAZY ABOUT THE IDEA AT FIRST, EITHER-- AND I'M NOT SAYING KUVIRA WOULD BE A PART OF OUR TEAM--BUT WITH HER HELP, WE CAN AVOID ANOTHER ALL-OUT BATTLE...
...AND PUT AN END TO THE EARTH EMPIRE, ***ONCE AND FOR ALL.***
BUT KUVIRA'S THE WORST. SHE THREATENED MY LIFE! MORE THAN ONCE!
I ALMOST LOST MY ARM TAKING OUT HER MECHA GIANT'S ENGINE.

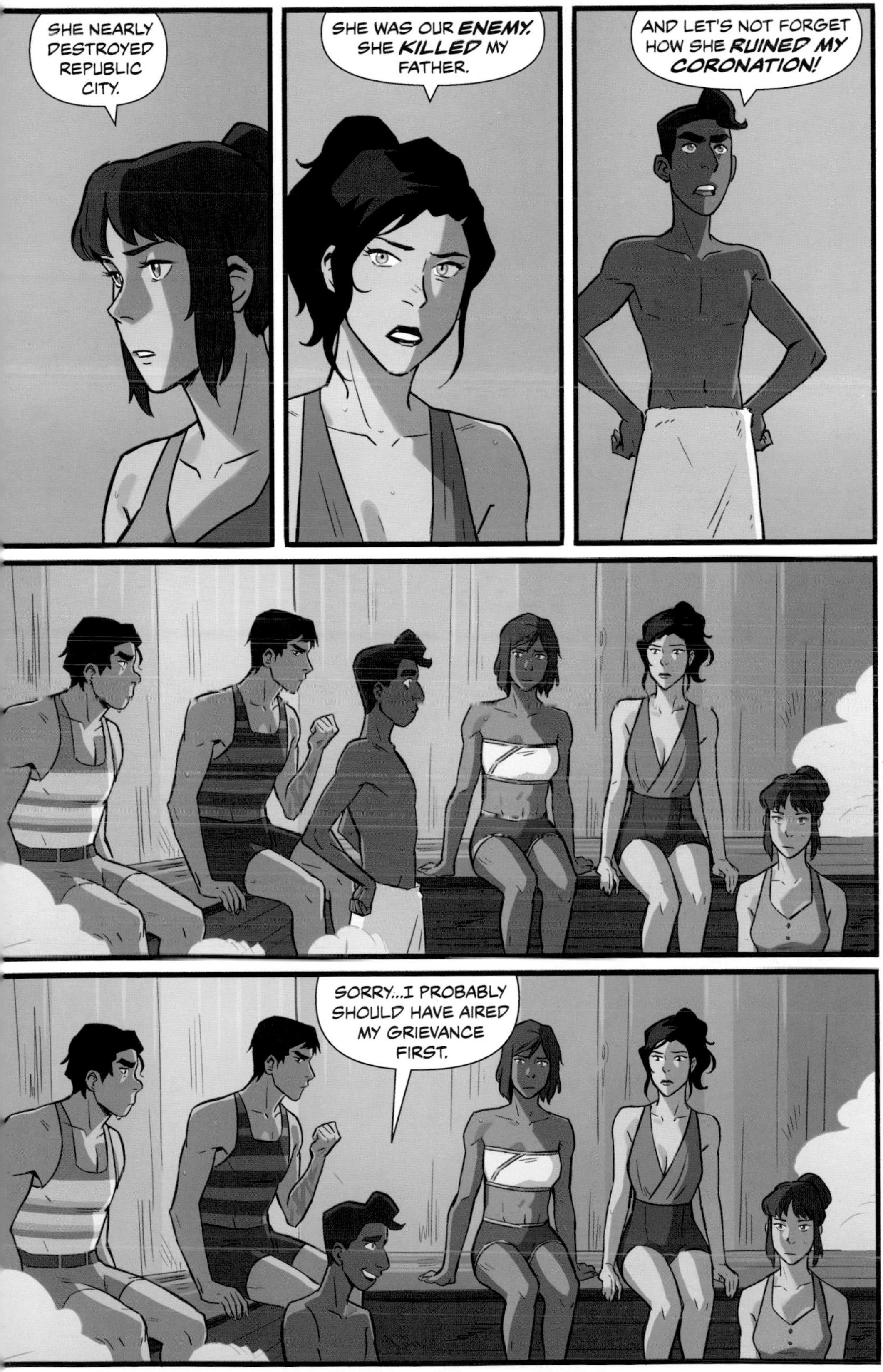
SHE NEARLY DESTROYED REPUBLIC CITY.
SHE WAS OUR ENEMY. SHE KILLED MY FATHER.
AND LET'S NOT FORGET HOW SHE RUINED MY CORONATION!
SORRY...I PROBABLY SHOULD HAVE AIRED MY GRIEVANCE FIRST.

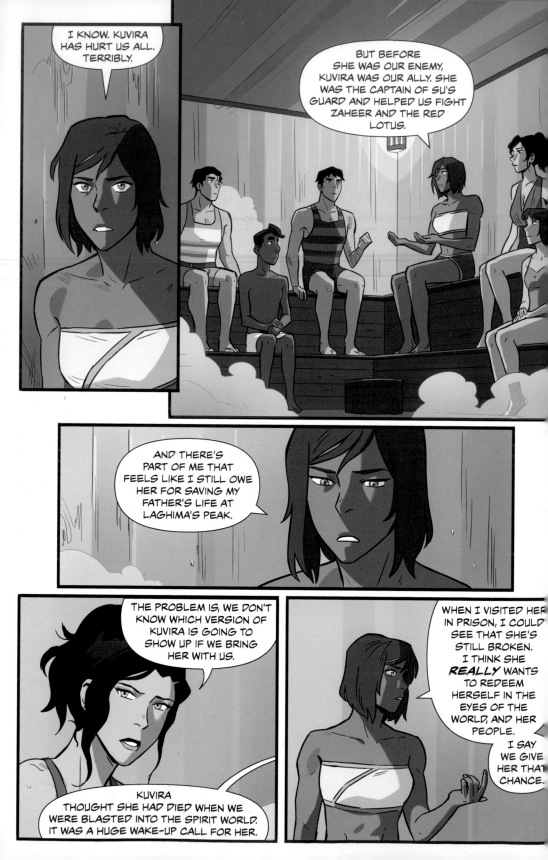

I KNOW. KUVIRA HAS HURT US ALL. TERRIBLY.

BUT BEFORE SHE WAS OUR ENEMY, KUVIRA WAS OUR ALLY. SHE WAS THE CAPTAIN OF SU'S GUARD AND HELPED US FIGHT ZAHEER AND THE RED LOTUS.

AND THERE'S PART OF ME THAT FEELS LIKE I STILL OWE HER FOR SAVING MY FATHER'S LIFE AT LAGHIMA'S PEAK.

THE PROBLEM IS, WE DON'T KNOW WHICH VERSION OF KUVIRA IS GOING TO SHOW UP IF WE BRING HER WITH US.

KUVIRA THOUGHT SHE HAD DIED WHEN WE WERE BLASTED INTO THE SPIRIT WORLD. IT WAS A HUGE WAKE-UP CALL FOR HER.

WHEN I VISITED HER IN PRISON, I COULD SEE THAT SHE'S STILL BROKEN. I THINK SHE *REALLY* WANTS TO REDEEM HERSELF IN THE EYES OF THE WORLD, AND HER PEOPLE.

I SAY WE GIVE HER THAT CHANCE.

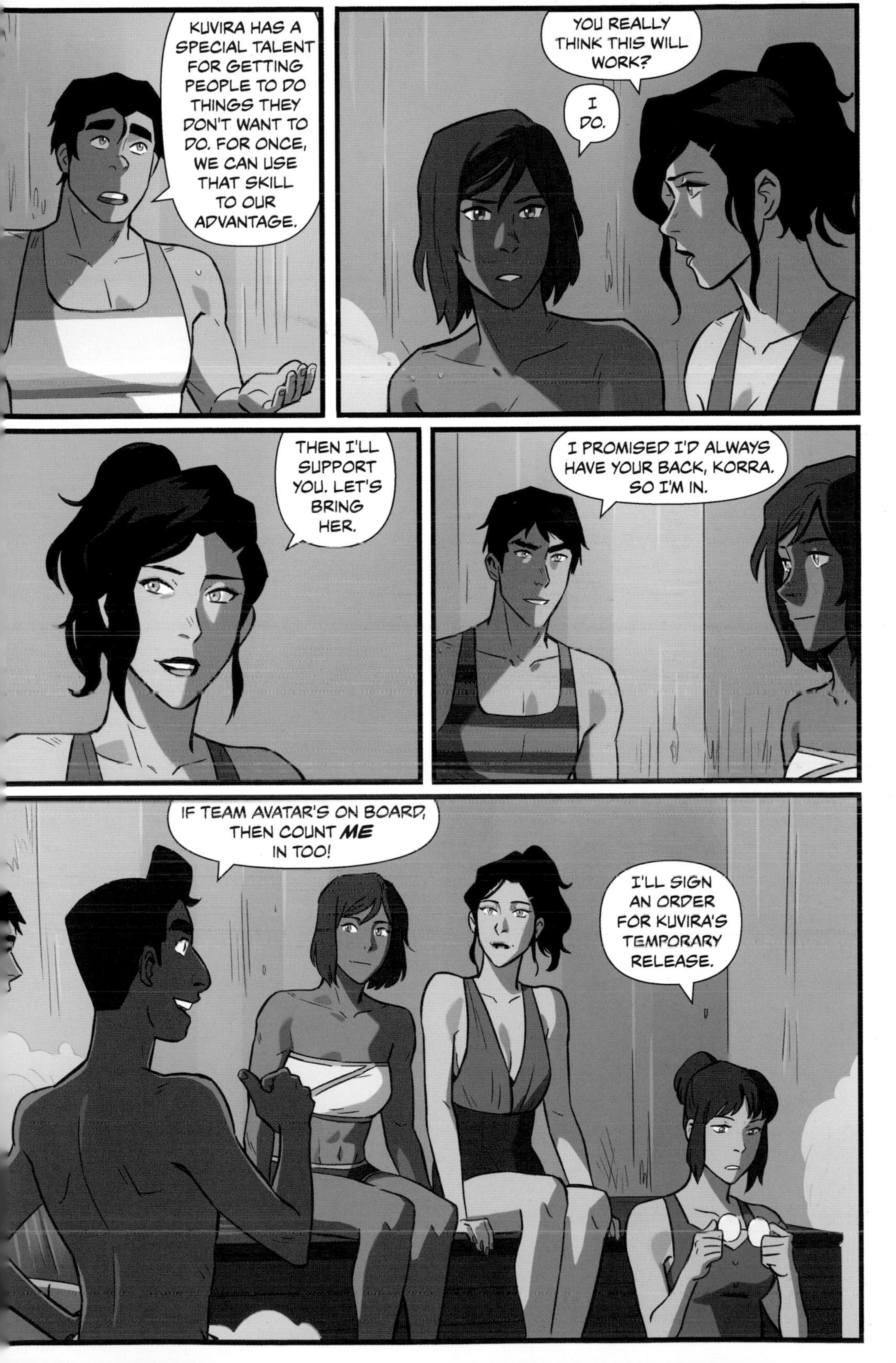
KUVIRA HAS A SPECIAL TALENT FOR GETTING PEOPLE TO DO THINGS THEY DON'T WANT TO DO. FOR ONCE, WE CAN USE THAT SKILL TO OUR ADVANTAGE.
YOU REALLY THINK THIS WILL WORK?
I DO.
THEN I'LL SUPPORT YOU. LET'S BRING HER.
I PROMISED I'D ALWAYS HAVE YOUR BACK, KORRA. SO I'M IN.
IF TEAM AVATAR'S ON BOARD, THEN COUNT ***ME*** IN TOO!
I'LL SIGN AN ORDER FOR KUVIRA'S TEMPORARY RELEASE.

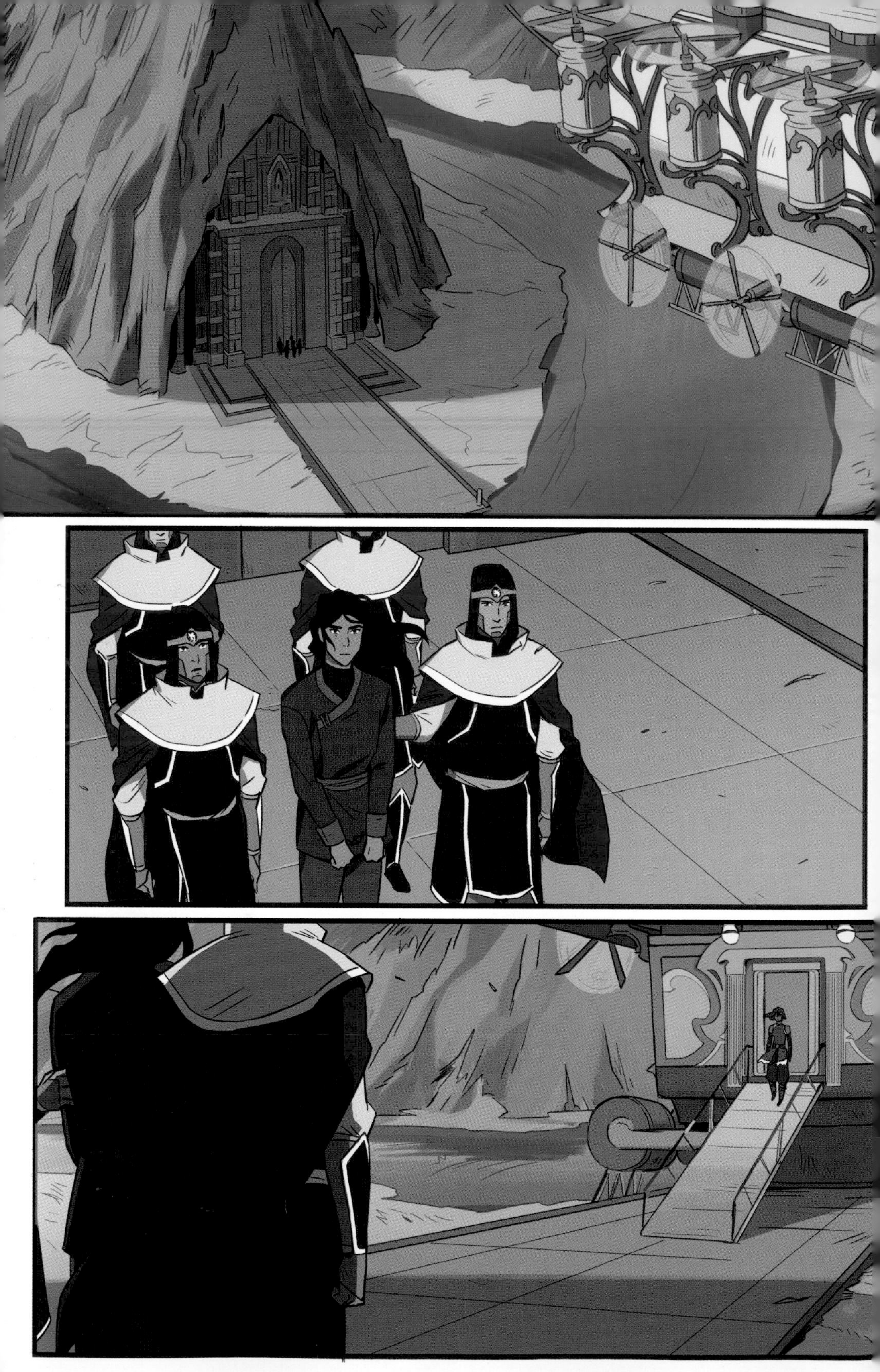

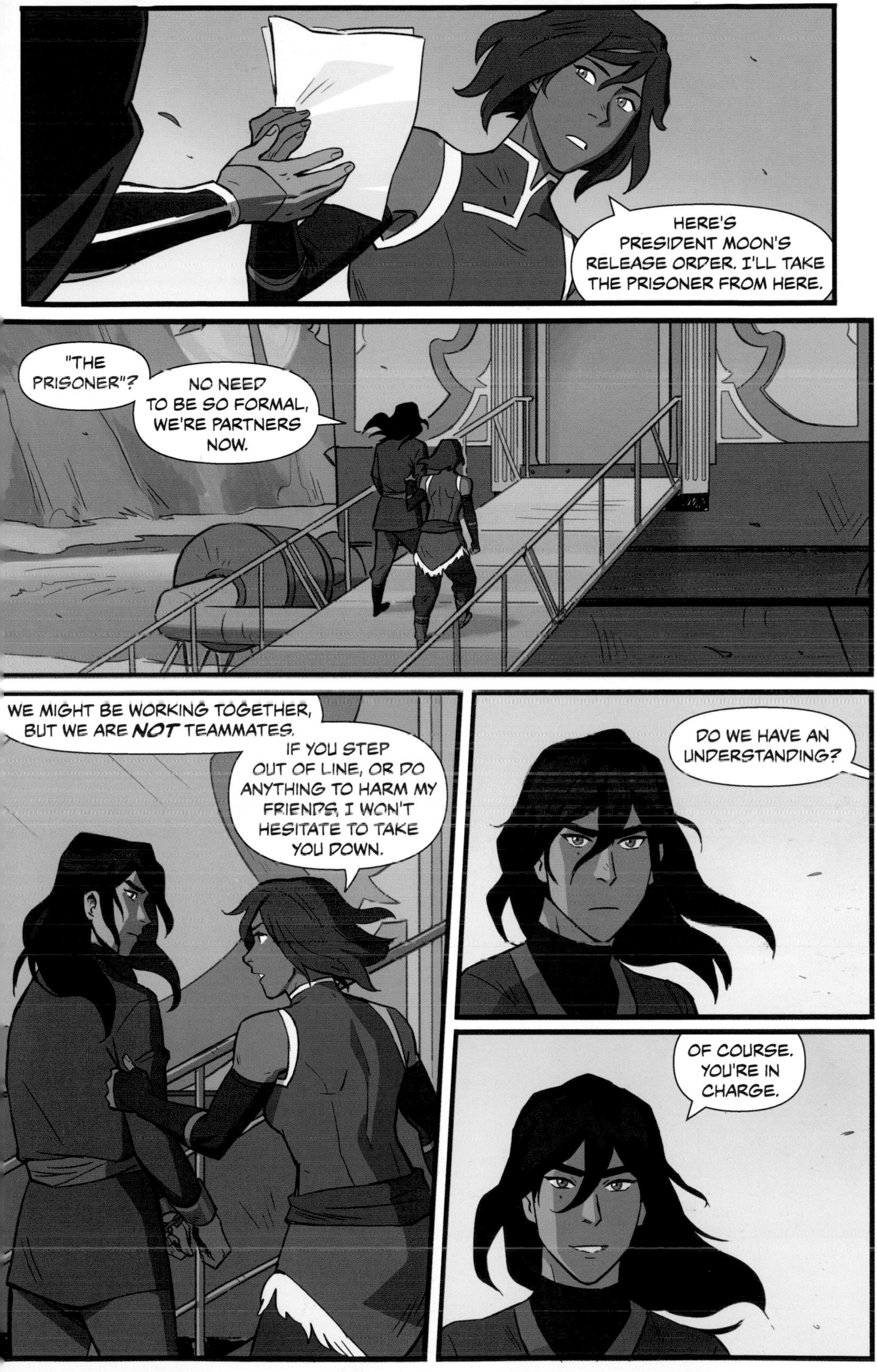
HERE'S PRESIDENT MOON'S RELEASE ORDER. I'LL TAKE THE PRISONER FROM HERE.
"THE PRISONER"?
NO NEED TO BE SO FORMAL, WE'RE PARTNERS NOW.
WE MIGHT BE WORKING TOGETHER, BUT WE ARE **NOT** TEAMMATES.
IF YOU STEP OUT OF LINE, OR DO ANYTHING TO HARM MY FRIENDS, I WON'T HESITATE TO TAKE YOU DOWN.
DO WE HAVE AN UNDERSTANDING?
OF COURSE. YOU'RE IN CHARGE.

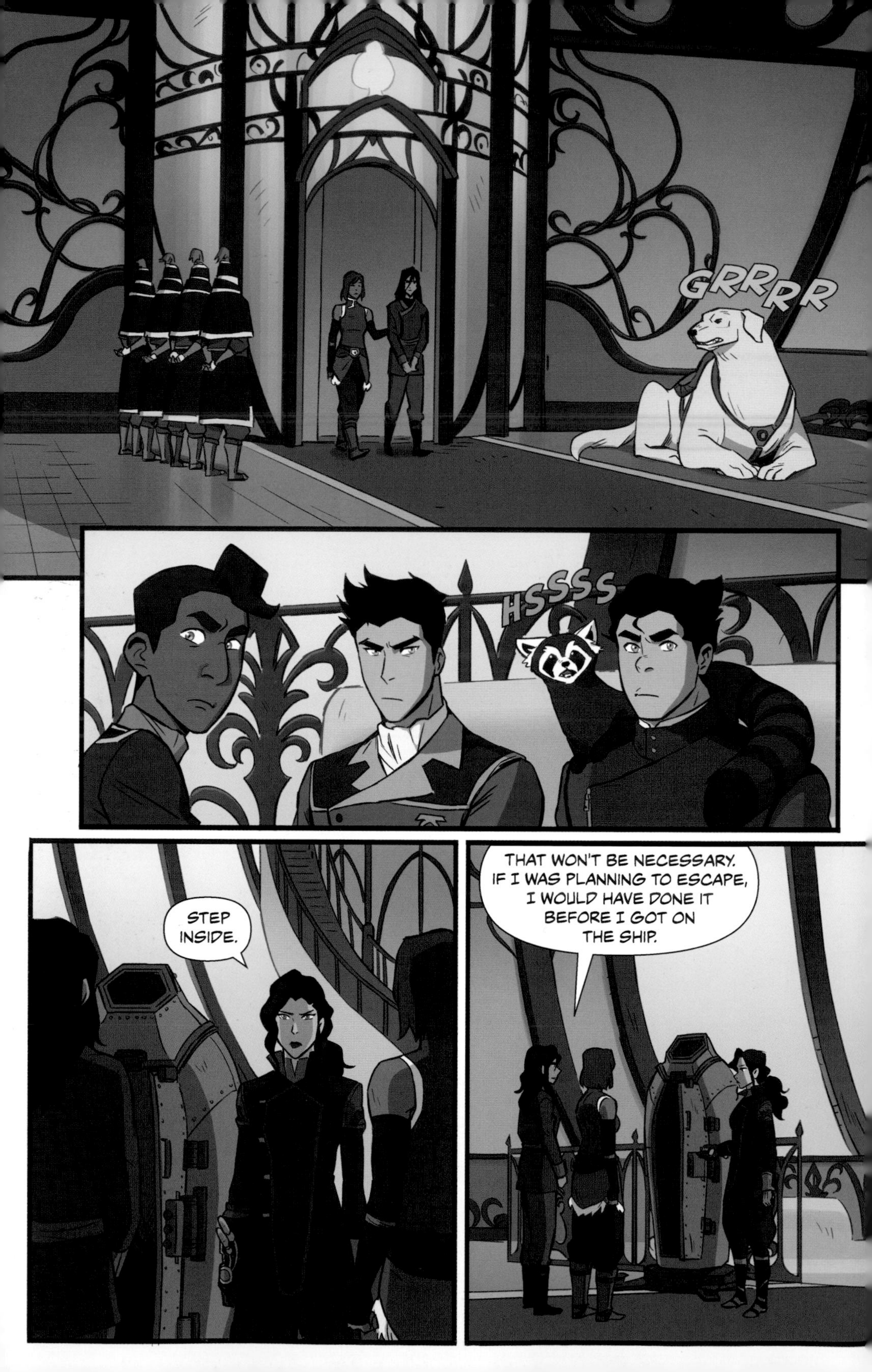
GRRRR
HSSSS
STEP INSIDE.
THAT WON'T BE NECESSARY. IF I WAS PLANNING TO ESCAPE, I WOULD HAVE DONE IT BEFORE I GOT ON THE SHIP.

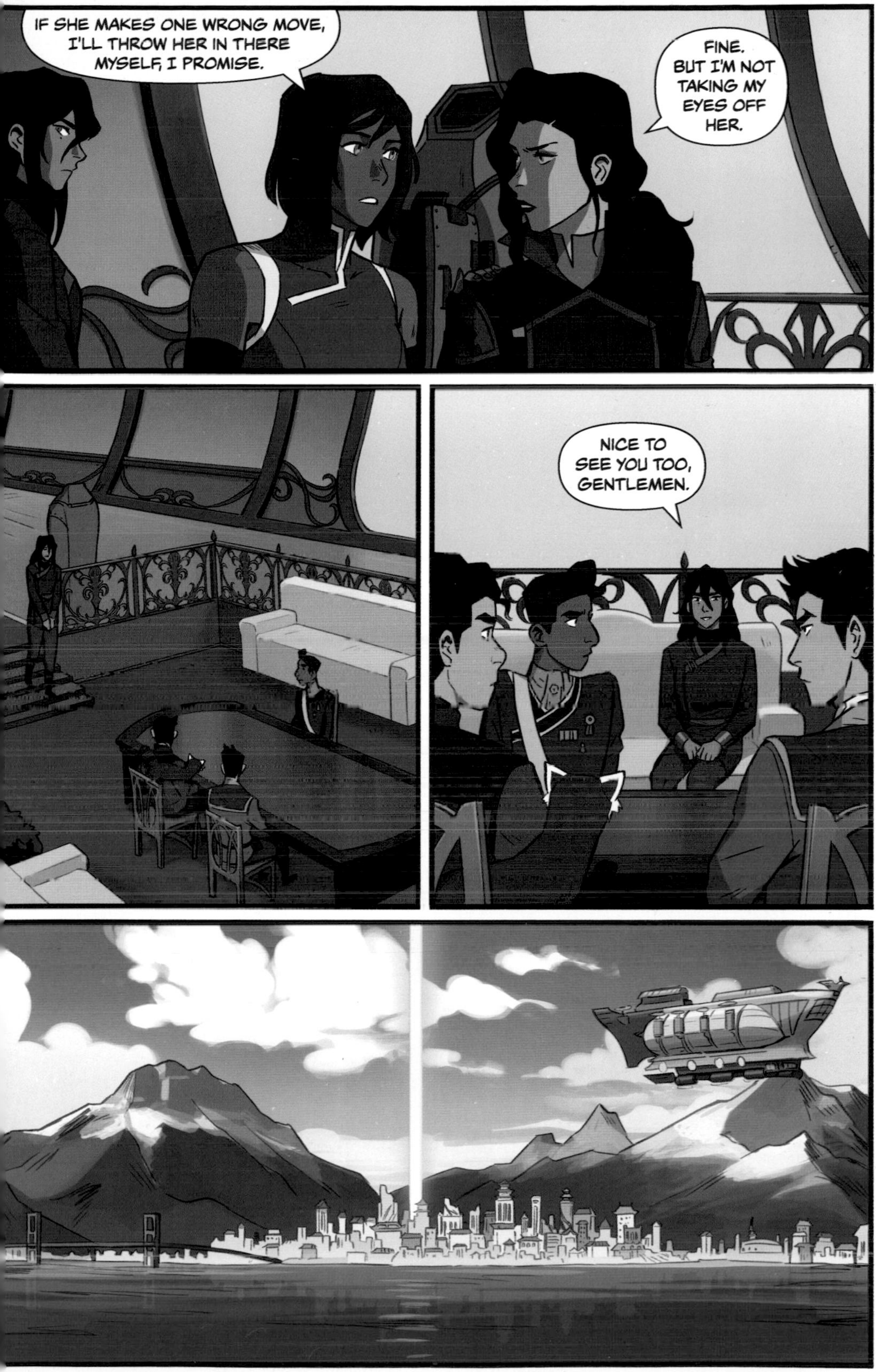
IF SHE MAKES ONE WRONG MOVE, I'LL THROW HER IN THERE MYSELF, I PROMISE.
FINE. BUT I'M NOT TAKING MY EYES OFF HER.
NICE TO SEE YOU TOO, GENTLEMEN.

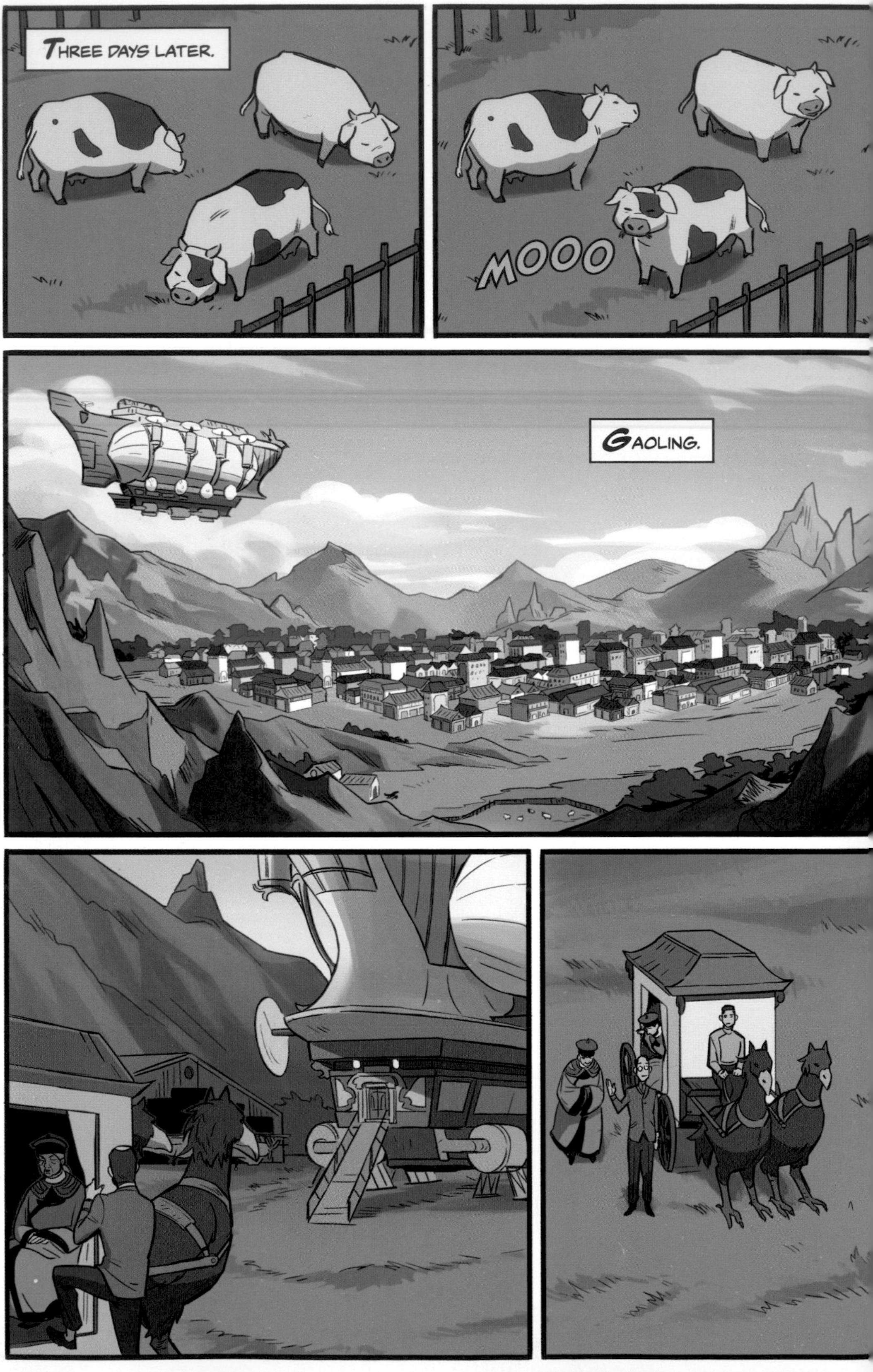
THREE DAYS LATER.
MOOO
GAOLING.

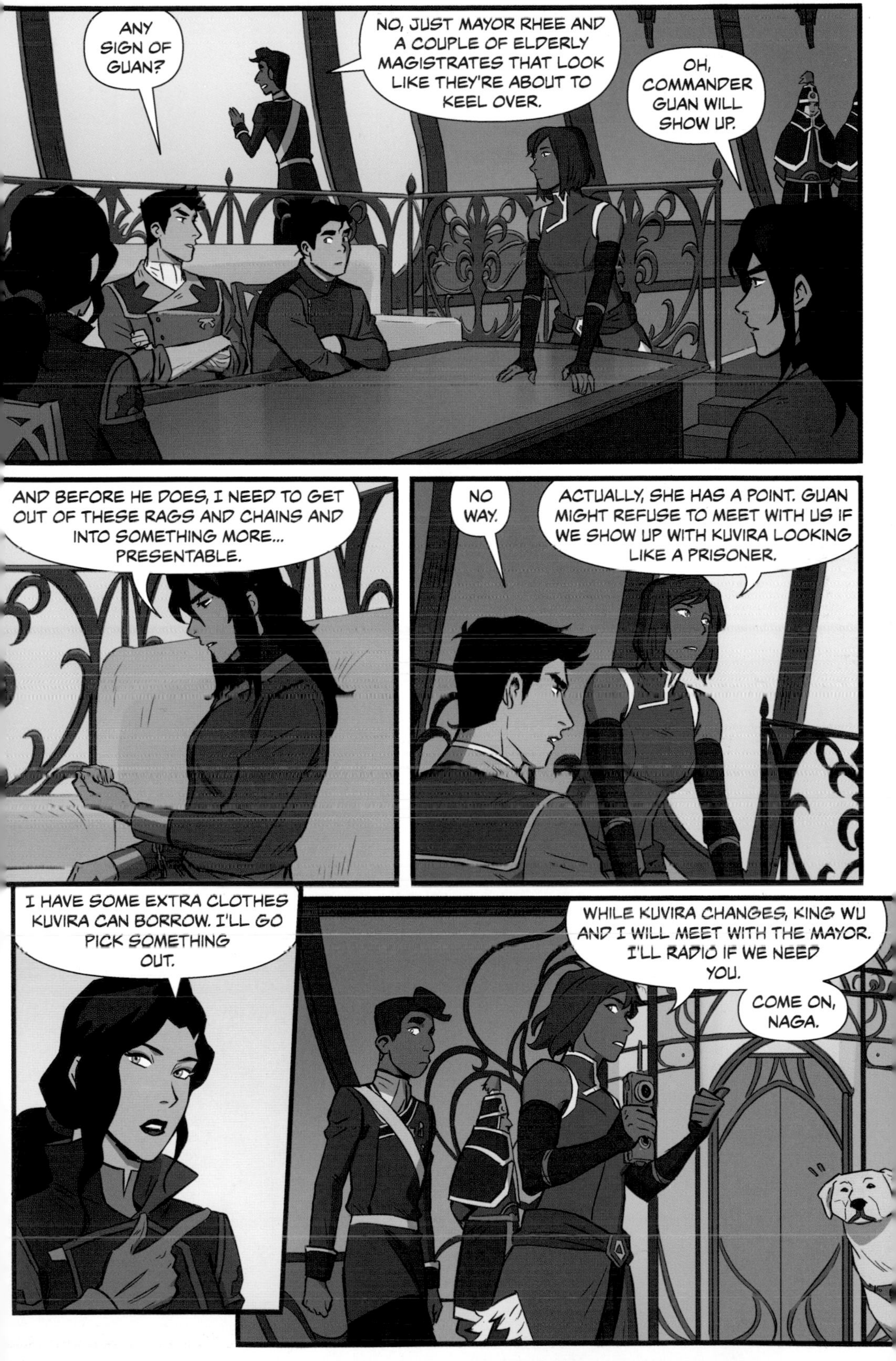
ANY SIGN OF GUAN?
NO, JUST MAYOR RHEE AND A COUPLE OF ELDERLY MAGISTRATES THAT LOOK LIKE THEY'RE ABOUT TO KEEL OVER.
OH, COMMANDER GUAN WILL SHOW UP.
AND BEFORE HE DOES, I NEED TO GET OUT OF THESE RAGS AND CHAINS AND INTO SOMETHING MORE... PRESENTABLE.
NO WAY.
ACTUALLY, SHE HAS A POINT. GUAN MIGHT REFUSE TO MEET WITH US IF WE SHOW UP WITH KUVIRA LOOKING LIKE A PRISONER.
I HAVE SOME EXTRA CLOTHES KUVIRA CAN BORROW. I'LL GO PICK SOMETHING OUT.
WHILE KUVIRA CHANGES, KING WU AND I WILL MEET WITH THE MAYOR. I'LL RADIO IF WE NEED YOU.
COME ON, NAGA.

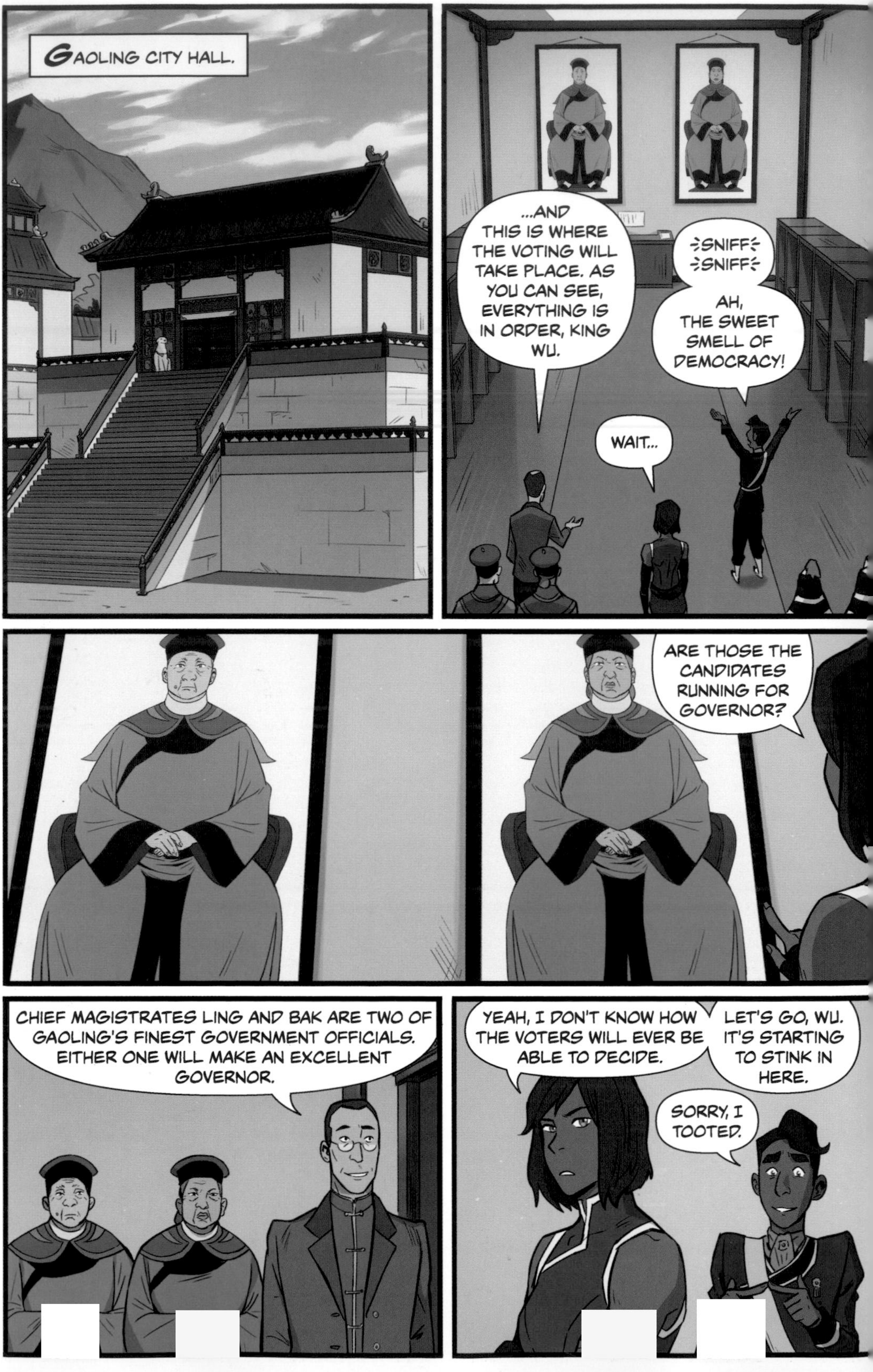
GAOLING CITY HALL.
...AND THIS IS WHERE THE VOTING WILL TAKE PLACE. AS YOU CAN SEE, EVERYTHING IS IN ORDER, KING WU.
SNIFF SNIFF
AH, THE SWEET SMELL OF DEMOCRACY!
WAIT...
ARE THOSE THE CANDIDATES RUNNING FOR GOVERNOR?
CHIEF MAGISTRATES LING AND BAK ARE TWO OF GAOLING'S FINEST GOVERNMENT OFFICIALS. EITHER ONE WILL MAKE AN EXCELLENT GOVERNOR.
YEAH, I DON'T KNOW HOW THE VOTERS WILL EVER BE ABLE TO DECIDE.
LET'S GO, WU. IT'S STARTING TO STINK IN HERE.
SORRY, I TOOTED.

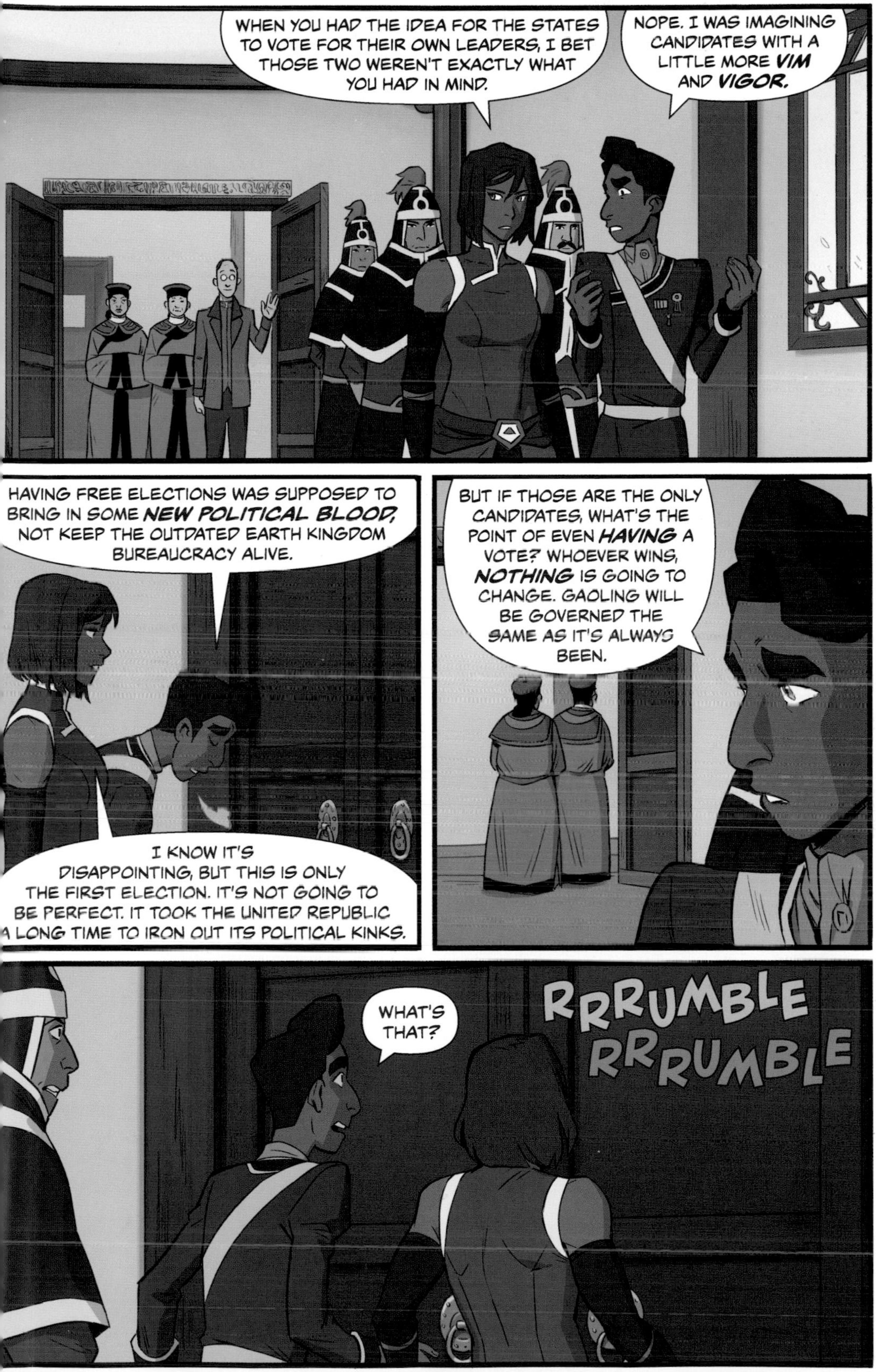
WHEN YOU HAD THE IDEA FOR THE STATES TO VOTE FOR THEIR OWN LEADERS, I BET THOSE TWO WEREN'T EXACTLY WHAT YOU HAD IN MIND.
NOPE. I WAS IMAGINING CANDIDATES WITH A LITTLE MORE VIM AND VIGOR.
HAVING FREE ELECTIONS WAS SUPPOSED TO BRING IN SOME NEW POLITICAL BLOOD, NOT KEEP THE OUTDATED EARTH KINGDOM BUREAUCRACY ALIVE.
I KNOW IT'S DISAPPOINTING, BUT THIS IS ONLY THE FIRST ELECTION. IT'S NOT GOING TO BE PERFECT. IT TOOK THE UNITED REPUBLIC A LONG TIME TO IRON OUT ITS POLITICAL KINKS.
BUT IF THOSE ARE THE ONLY CANDIDATES, WHAT'S THE POINT OF EVEN HAVING A VOTE? WHOEVER WINS, NOTHING IS GOING TO CHANGE. GAOLING WILL BE GOVERNED THE SAME AS IT'S ALWAYS BEEN.
WHAT'S THAT?
RRRUMBLE
RRRUMBLE

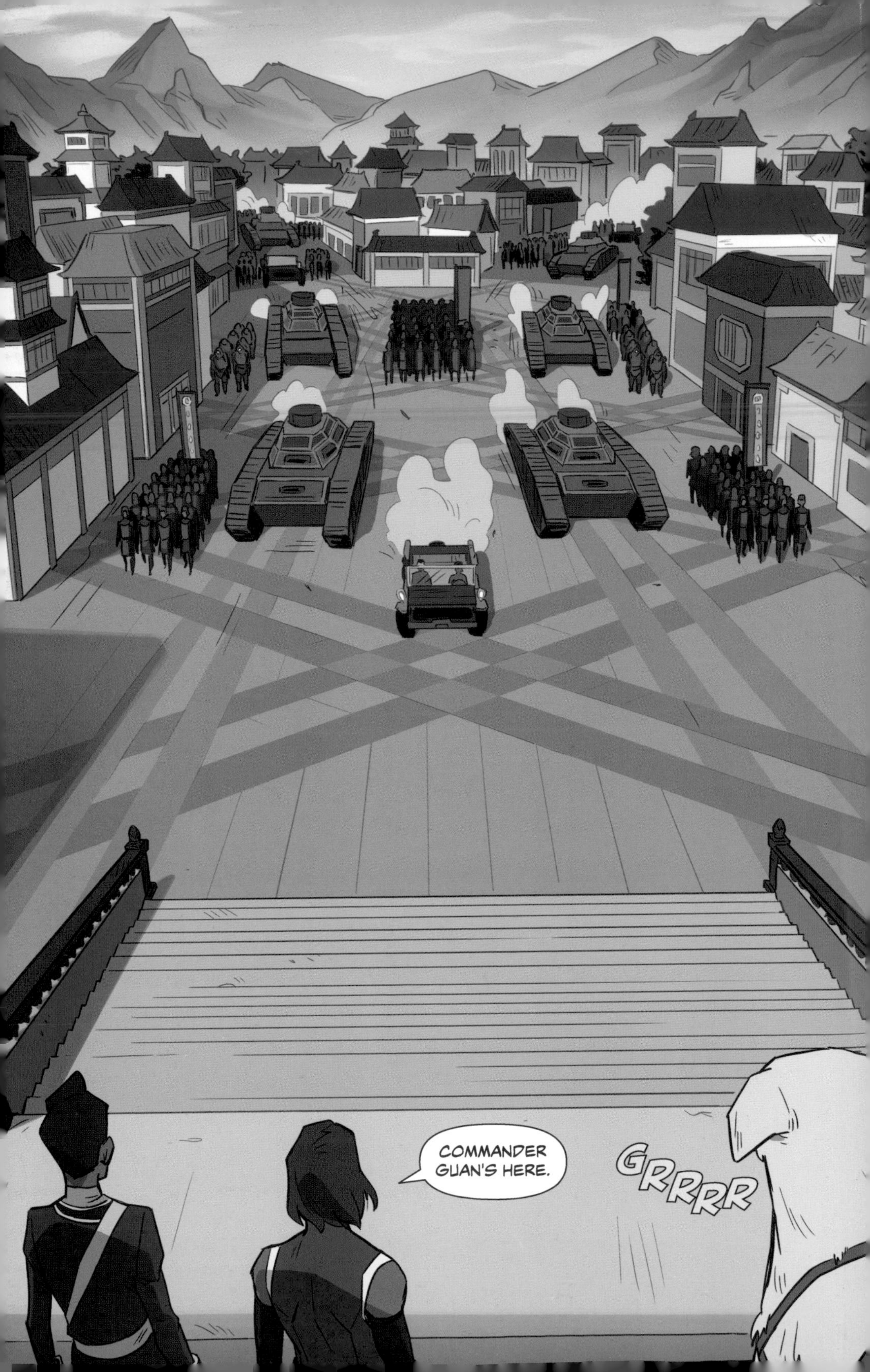
COMMANDER GUAN'S HERE.
GRRRR

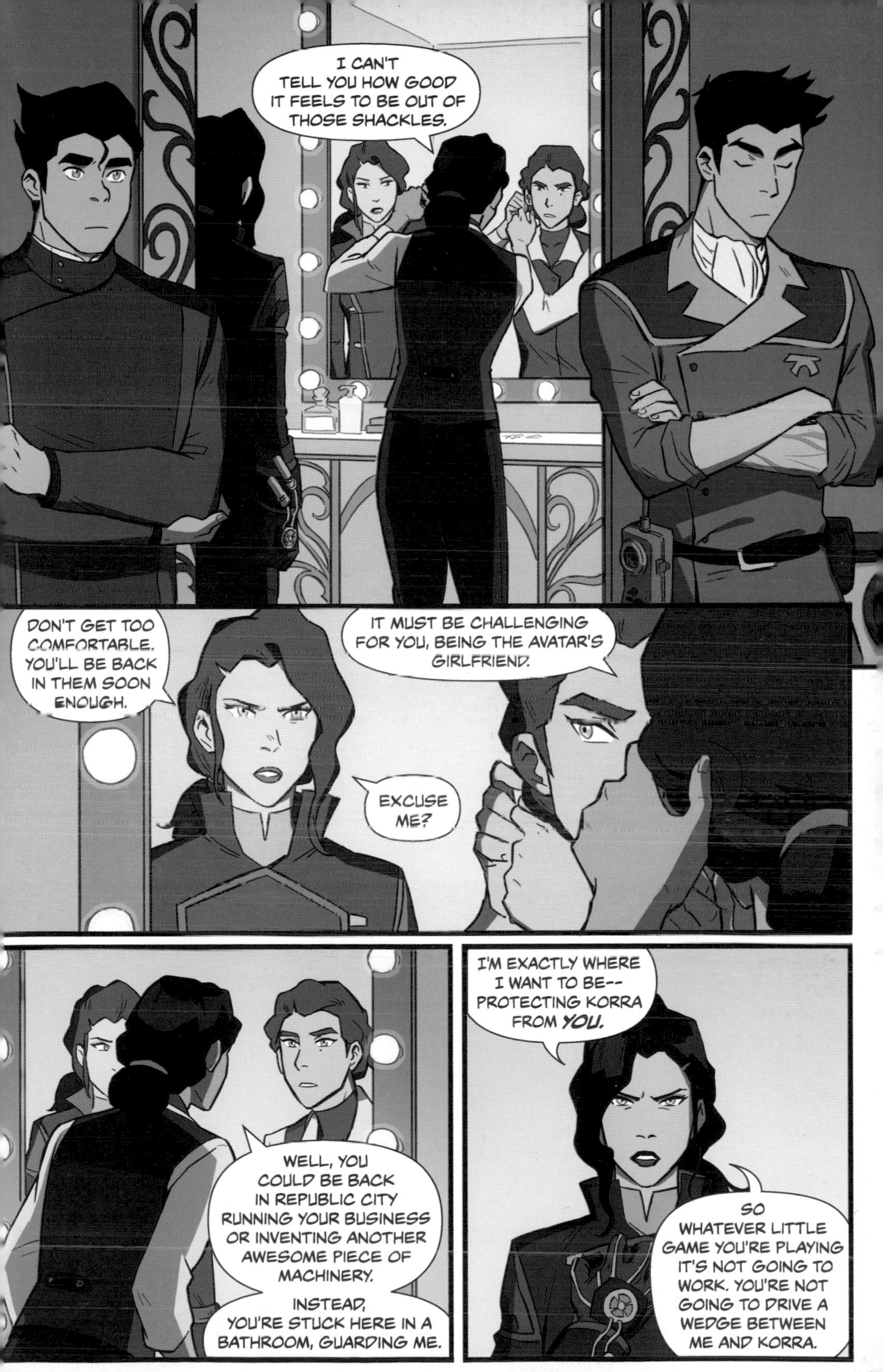

I CAN'T TELL YOU HOW GOOD IT FEELS TO BE OUT OF THOSE SHACKLES.
DON'T GET TOO COMFORTABLE. YOU'LL BE BACK IN THEM SOON ENOUGH.
IT MUST BE CHALLENGING FOR YOU, BEING THE AVATAR'S GIRLFRIEND.
EXCUSE ME?
WELL, YOU COULD BE BACK IN REPUBLIC CITY RUNNING YOUR BUSINESS OR INVENTING ANOTHER AWESOME PIECE OF MACHINERY.
INSTEAD, YOU'RE STUCK HERE IN A BATHROOM, GUARDING ME.
I'M EXACTLY WHERE I WANT TO BE-- PROTECTING KORRA FROM YOU.
SO WHATEVER LITTLE GAME YOU'RE PLAYING IT'S NOT GOING TO WORK. YOU'RE NOT GOING TO DRIVE A WEDGE BETWEEN ME AND KORRA.

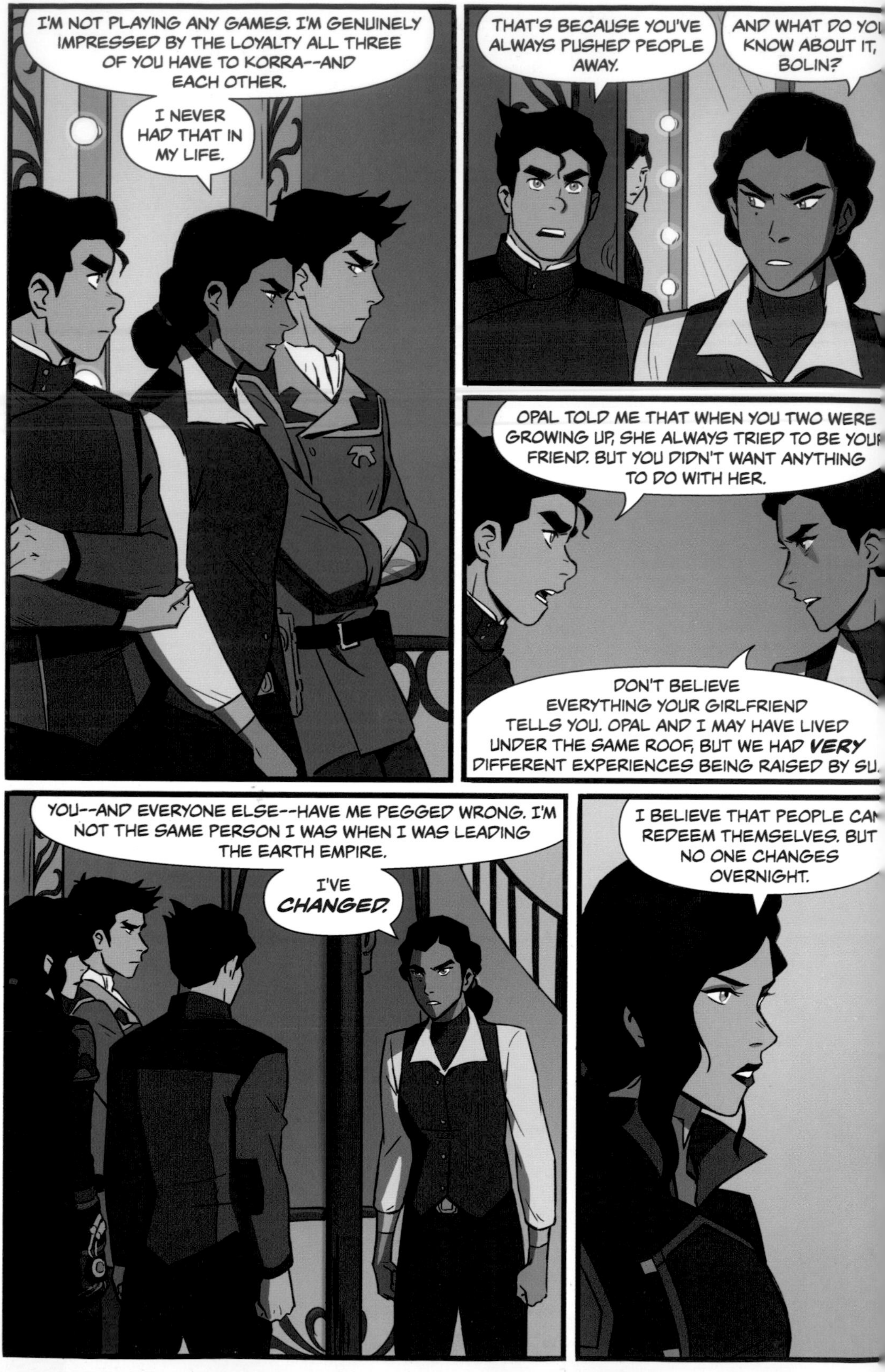
I'M NOT PLAYING ANY GAMES. I'M GENUINELY IMPRESSED BY THE LOYALTY ALL THREE OF YOU HAVE TO KORRA--AND EACH OTHER.
I NEVER HAD THAT IN MY LIFE.
THAT'S BECAUSE YOU'VE ALWAYS PUSHED PEOPLE AWAY.
AND WHAT DO YOU KNOW ABOUT IT, BOLIN?
OPAL TOLD ME THAT WHEN YOU TWO WERE GROWING UP, SHE ALWAYS TRIED TO BE YOUR FRIEND. BUT YOU DIDN'T WANT ANYTHING TO DO WITH HER.
DON'T BELIEVE EVERYTHING YOUR GIRLFRIEND TELLS YOU. OPAL AND I MAY HAVE LIVED UNDER THE SAME ROOF, BUT WE HAD VERY DIFFERENT EXPERIENCES BEING RAISED BY SU.
YOU--AND EVERYONE ELSE--HAVE ME PEGGED WRONG. I'M NOT THE SAME PERSON I WAS WHEN I WAS LEADING THE EARTH EMPIRE.
I'VE CHANGED.
I BELIEVE THAT PEOPLE CAN REDEEM THEMSELVES. BUT NO ONE CHANGES OVERNIGHT.

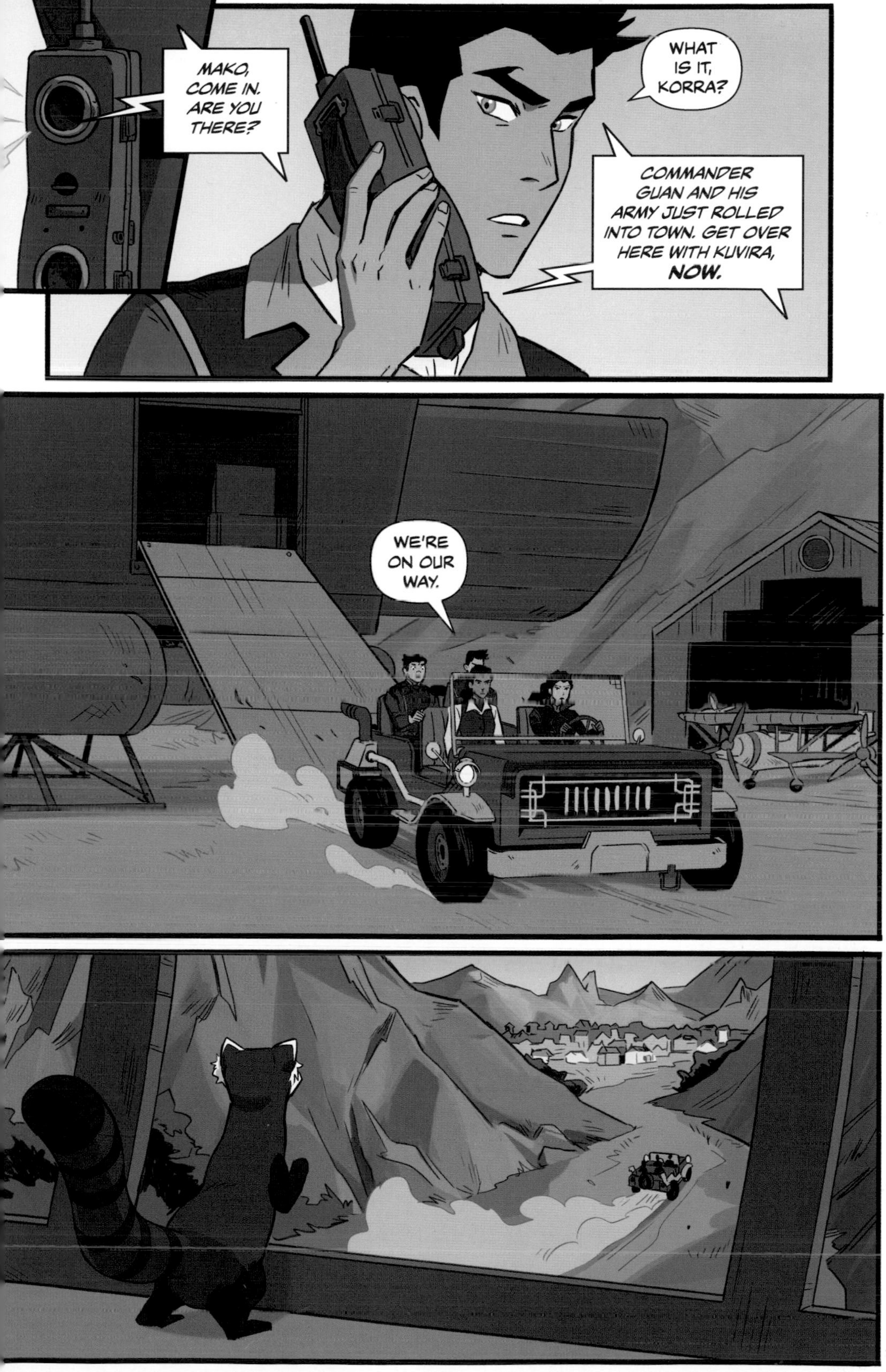
MAKO, COME IN. ARE YOU THERE?
WHAT IS IT, KORRA?
COMMANDER GUAN AND HIS ARMY JUST ROLLED INTO TOWN. GET OVER HERE WITH KUVIRA, NOW.
WE'RE ON OUR WAY.

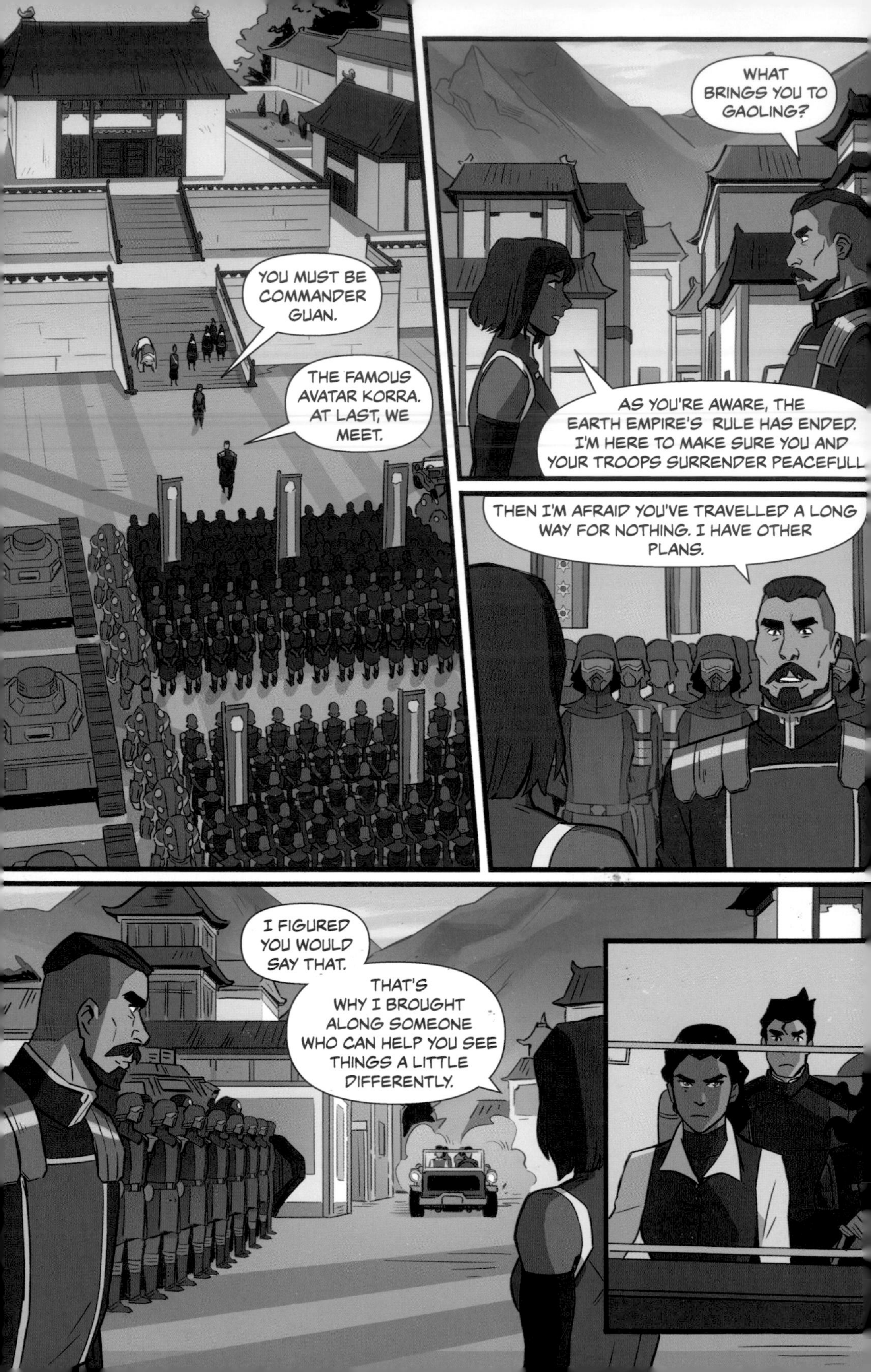
YOU MUST BE COMMANDER GUAN.
THE FAMOUS AVATAR KORRA. AT LAST, WE MEET.
WHAT BRINGS YOU TO GAOLING?
AS YOU'RE AWARE, THE EARTH EMPIRE'S RULE HAS ENDED. I'M HERE TO MAKE SURE YOU AND YOUR TROOPS SURRENDER PEACEFULL
THEN I'M AFRAID YOU'VE TRAVELLED A LONG WAY FOR NOTHING. I HAVE OTHER PLANS.
I FIGURED YOU WOULD SAY THAT.
THAT'S WHY I BROUGHT ALONG SOMEONE WHO CAN HELP YOU SEE THINGS A LITTLE DIFFERENTLY.

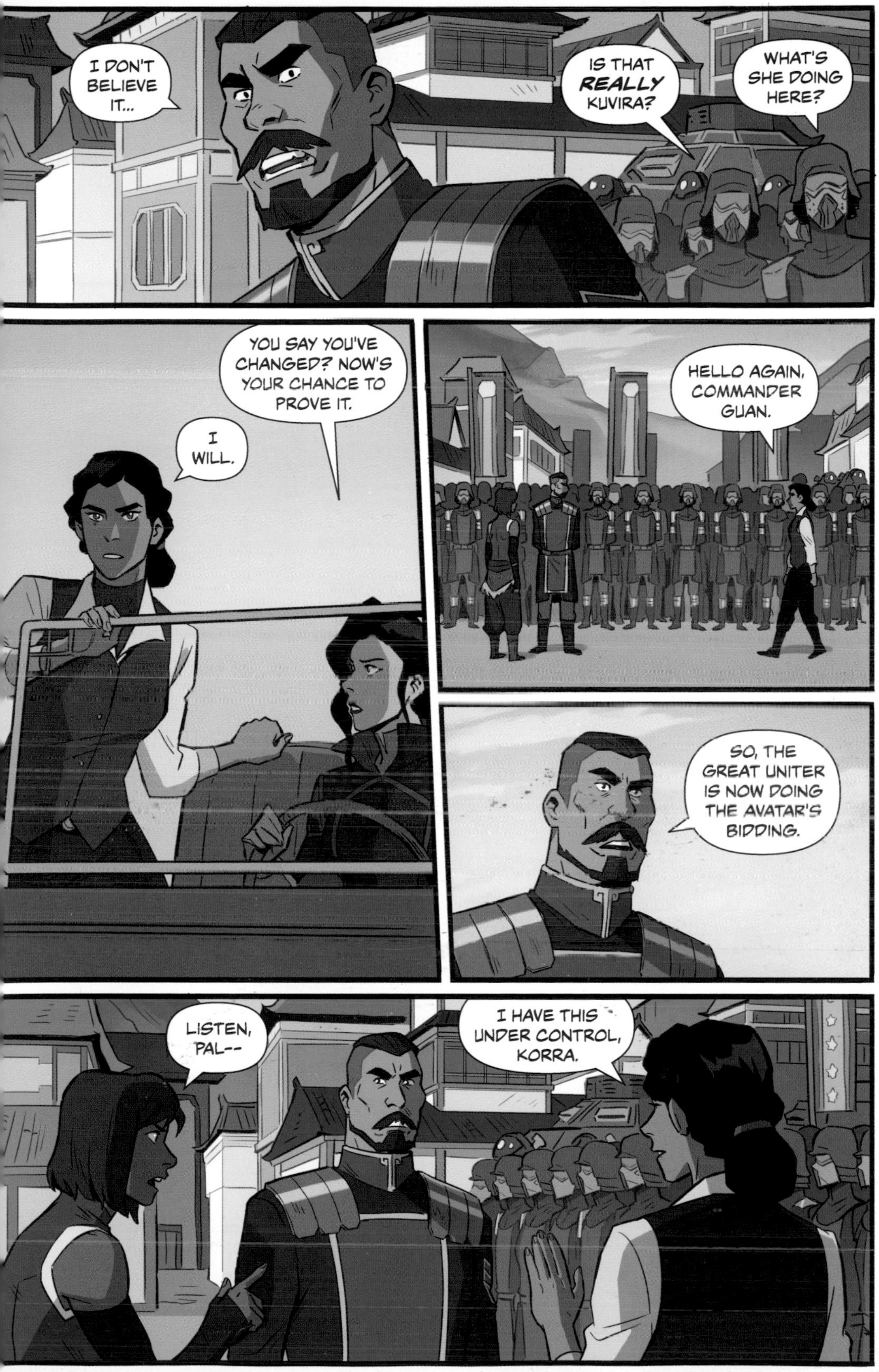
I DON'T BELIEVE IT...
IS THAT REALLY KUVIRA?
WHAT'S SHE DOING HERE?
YOU SAY YOU'VE CHANGED? NOW'S YOUR CHANCE TO PROVE IT.
I WILL.
HELLO AGAIN, COMMANDER GUAN.
SO, THE GREAT UNITER IS NOW DOING THE AVATAR'S BIDDING.
LISTEN, PAL--
I HAVE THIS UNDER CONTROL, KORRA.

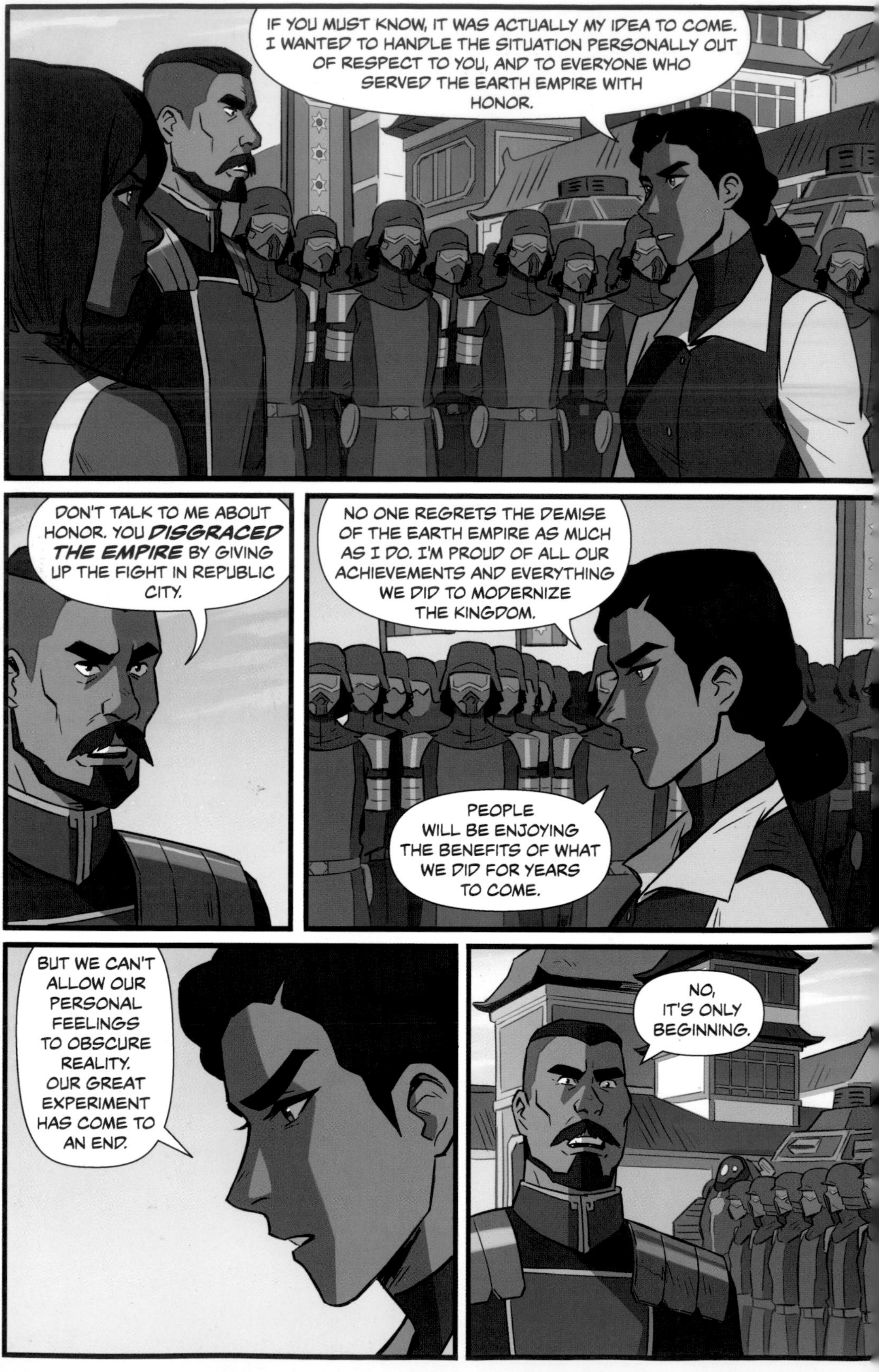
IF YOU MUST KNOW, IT WAS ACTUALLY MY IDEA TO COME. I WANTED TO HANDLE THE SITUATION PERSONALLY OUT OF RESPECT TO YOU, AND TO EVERYONE WHO SERVED THE EARTH EMPIRE WITH HONOR.
DON'T TALK TO ME ABOUT HONOR. YOU ***DISGRACED THE EMPIRE*** BY GIVING UP THE FIGHT IN REPUBLIC CITY.
NO ONE REGRETS THE DEMISE OF THE EARTH EMPIRE AS MUCH AS I DO. I'M PROUD OF ALL OUR ACHIEVEMENTS AND EVERYTHING WE DID TO MODERNIZE THE KINGDOM.
PEOPLE WILL BE ENJOYING THE BENEFITS OF WHAT WE DID FOR YEARS TO COME.
BUT WE CAN'T ALLOW OUR PERSONAL FEELINGS TO OBSCURE REALITY. OUR GREAT EXPERIMENT HAS COME TO AN END.
NO, IT'S ONLY BEGINNING.

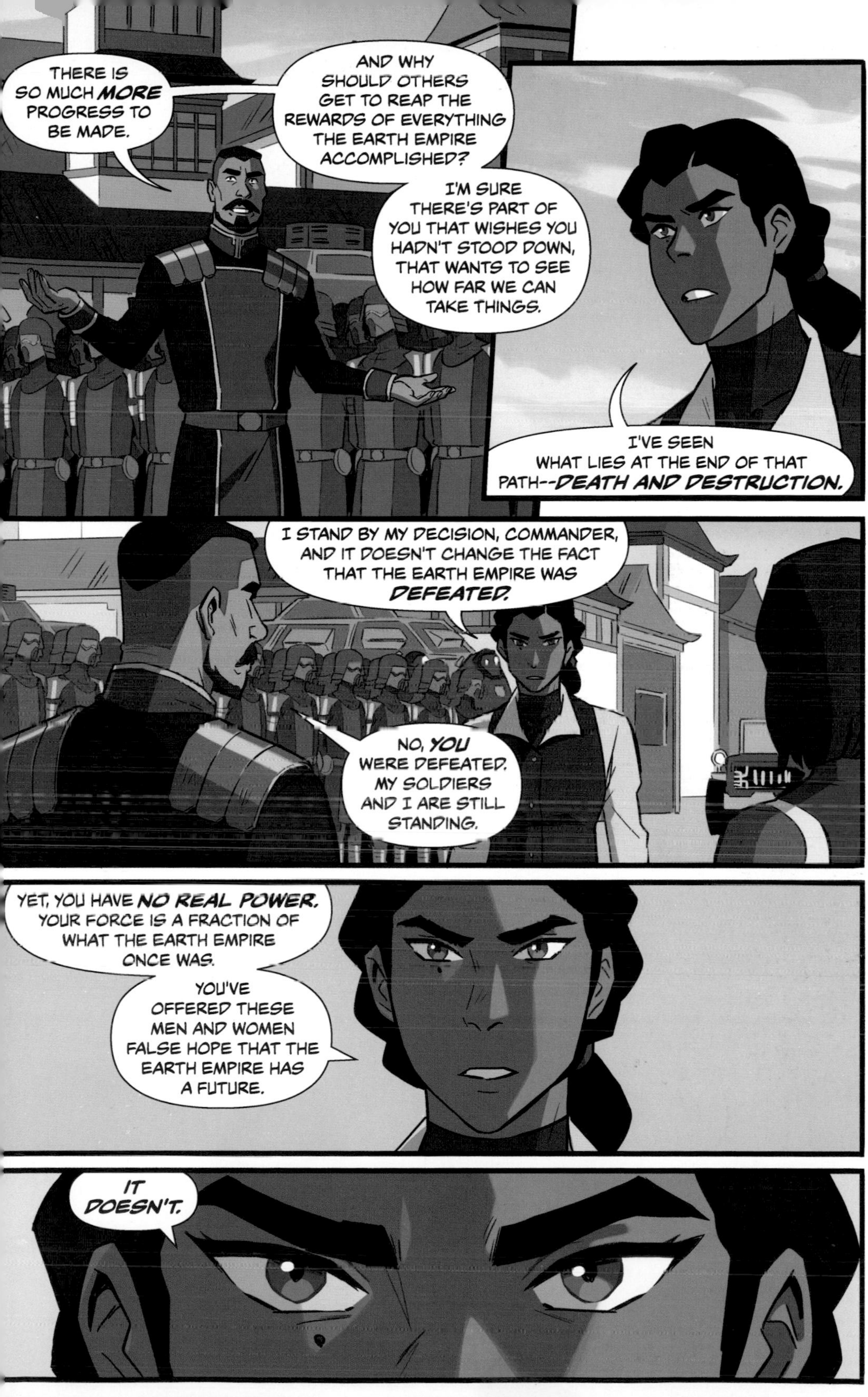
THERE IS SO MUCH MORE PROGRESS TO BE MADE.
AND WHY SHOULD OTHERS GET TO REAP THE REWARDS OF EVERYTHING THE EARTH EMPIRE ACCOMPLISHED?
I'M SURE THERE'S PART OF YOU THAT WISHES YOU HADN'T STOOD DOWN, THAT WANTS TO SEE HOW FAR WE CAN TAKE THINGS.
I'VE SEEN WHAT LIES AT THE END OF THAT PATH--DEATH AND DESTRUCTION.
I STAND BY MY DECISION, COMMANDER, AND IT DOESN'T CHANGE THE FACT THAT THE EARTH EMPIRE WAS DEFEATED.
NO, YOU WERE DEFEATED. MY SOLDIERS AND I ARE STILL STANDING.
YET, YOU HAVE NO REAL POWER. YOUR FORCE IS A FRACTION OF WHAT THE EARTH EMPIRE ONCE WAS.
YOU'VE OFFERED THESE MEN AND WOMEN FALSE HOPE THAT THE EARTH EMPIRE HAS A FUTURE.
IT DOESN'T.

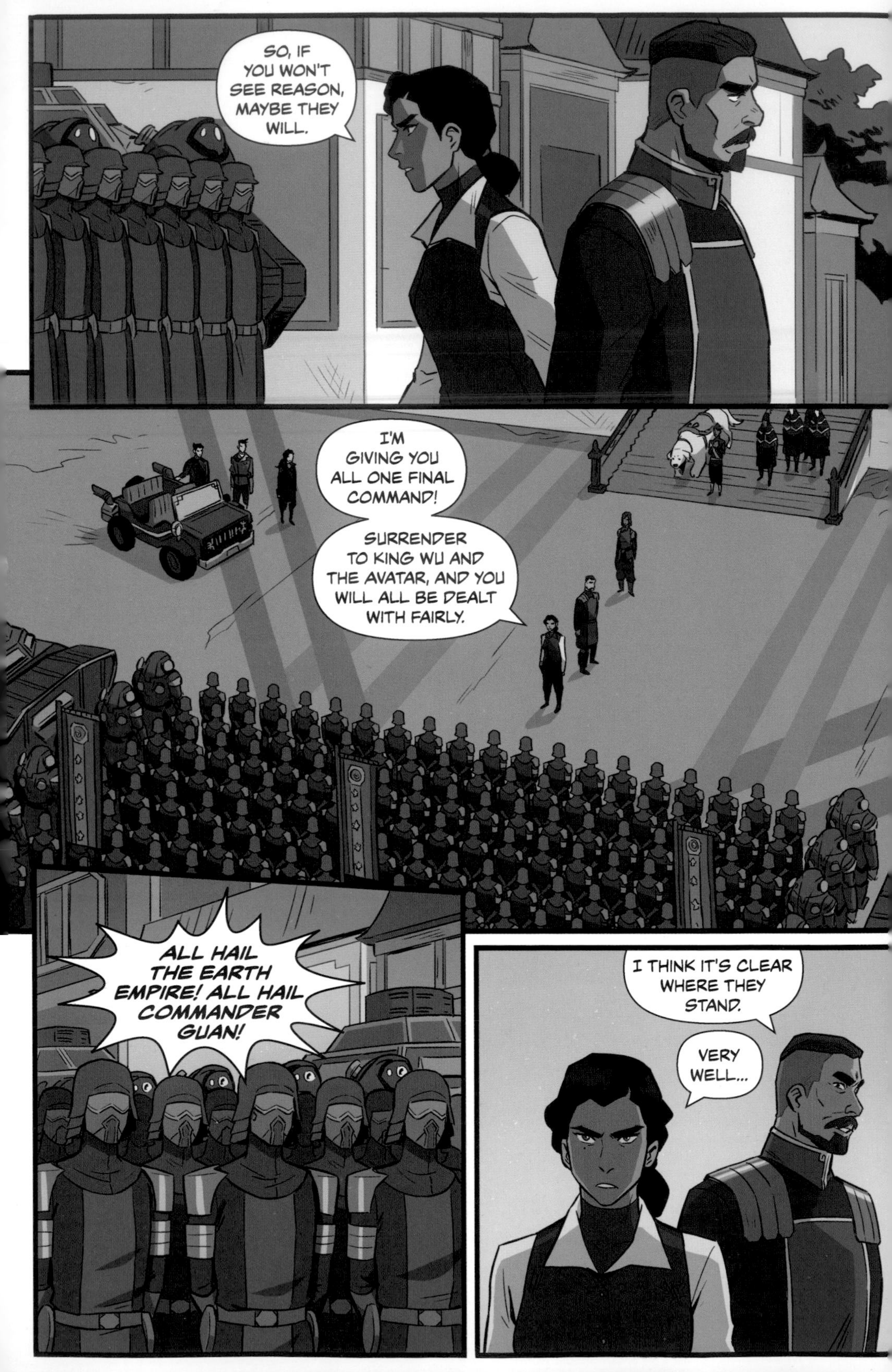
SO, IF YOU WON'T SEE REASON, MAYBE THEY WILL.
I'M GIVING YOU ALL ONE FINAL COMMAND!
SURRENDER TO KING WU AND THE AVATAR, AND YOU WILL ALL BE DEALT WITH FAIRLY.
ALL HAIL THE EARTH EMPIRE! ALL HAIL COMMANDER GUAN!
I THINK IT'S CLEAR WHERE THEY STAND.
VERY WELL...

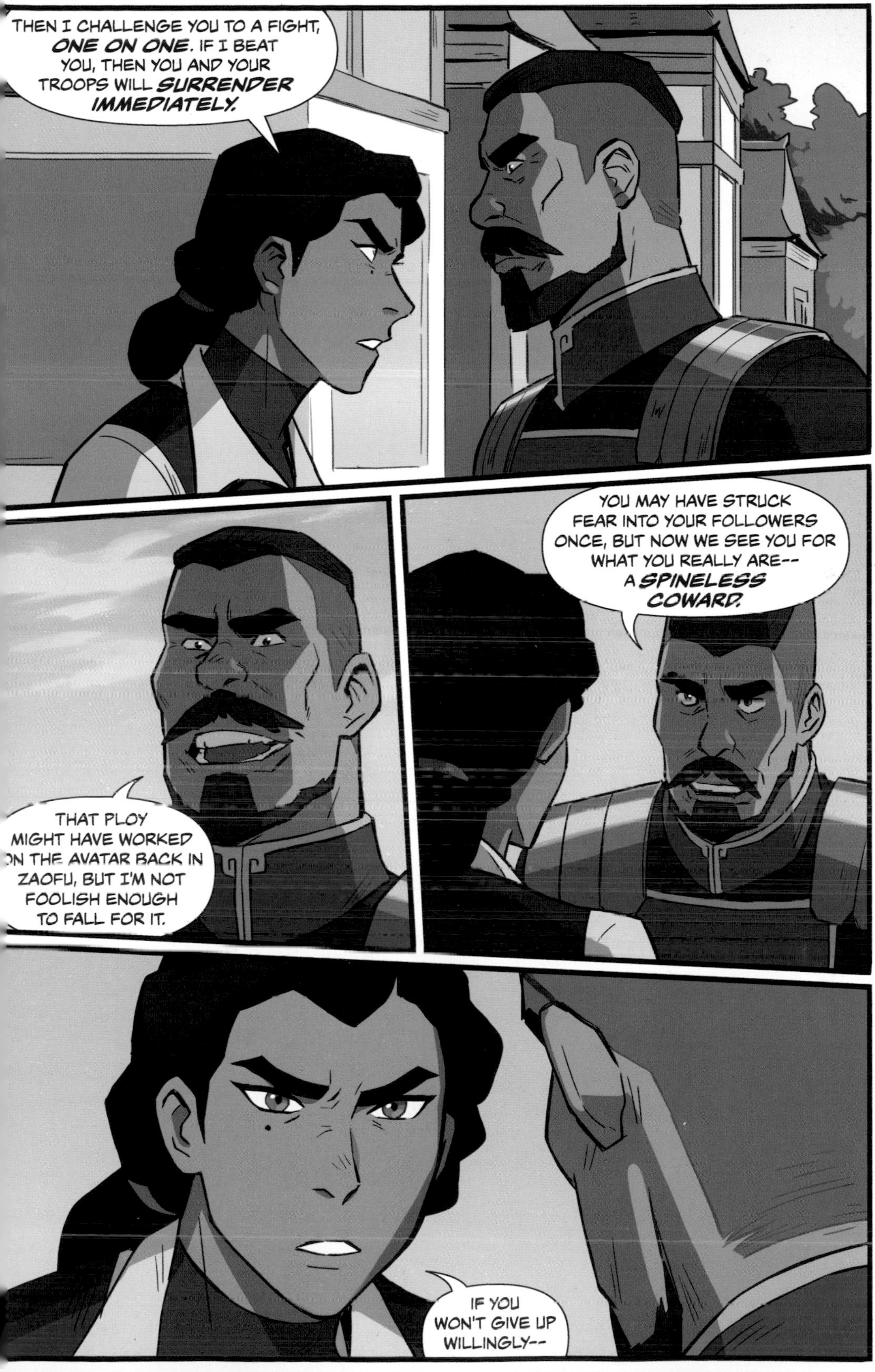
THEN I CHALLENGE YOU TO A FIGHT, ONE ON ONE. IF I BEAT YOU, THEN YOU AND YOUR TROOPS WILL SURRENDER IMMEDIATELY.
THAT PLOY MIGHT HAVE WORKED ON THE AVATAR BACK IN ZAOFU, BUT I'M NOT FOOLISH ENOUGH TO FALL FOR IT.
YOU MAY HAVE STRUCK FEAR INTO YOUR FOLLOWERS ONCE, BUT NOW WE SEE YOU FOR WHAT YOU REALLY ARE-- A SPINELESS COWARD.
IF YOU WON'T GIVE UP WILLINGLY--

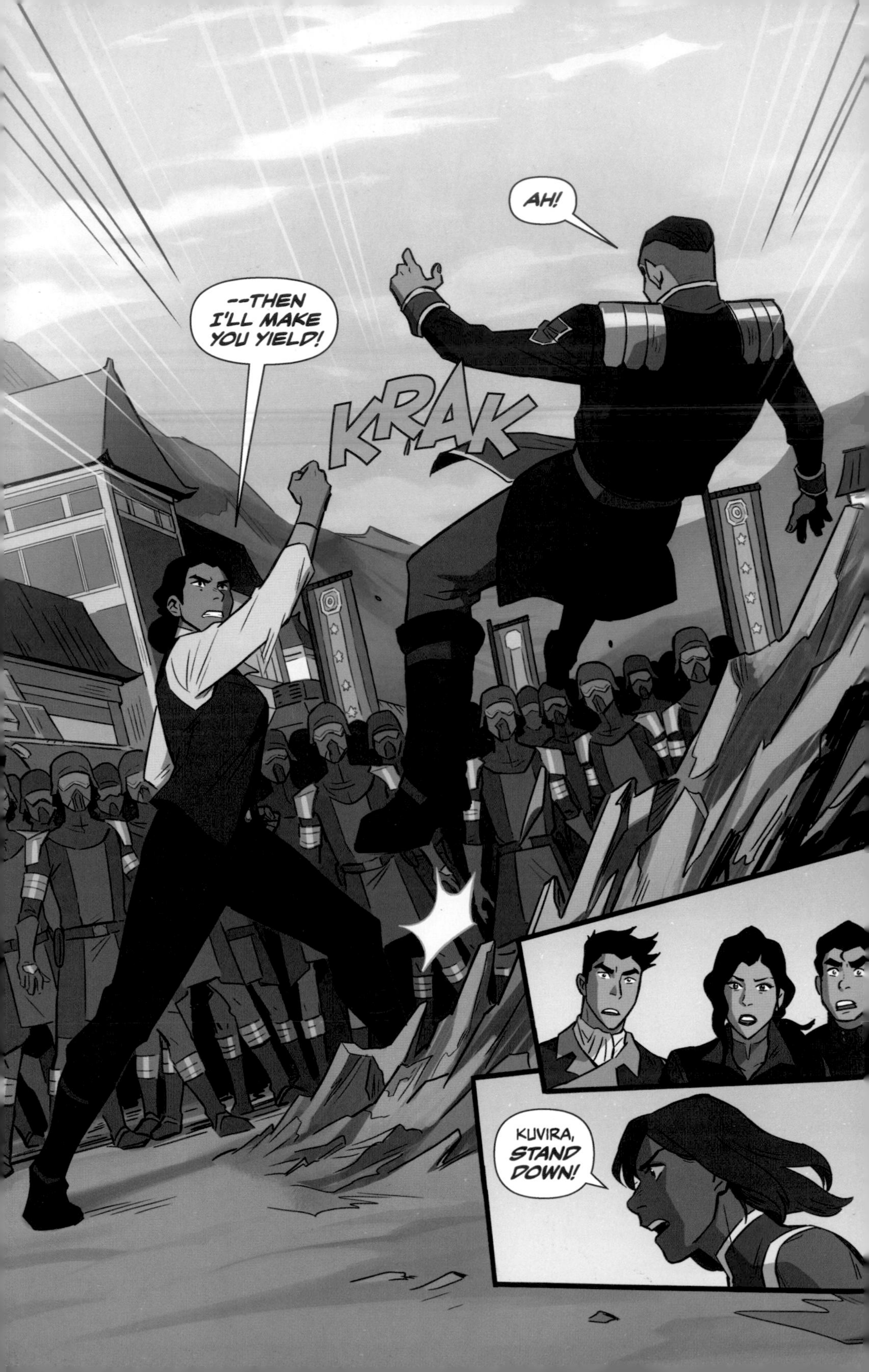
--THEN I'LL MAKE YOU YIELD!
AH!
KRAK
KUVIRA, STAND DOWN!

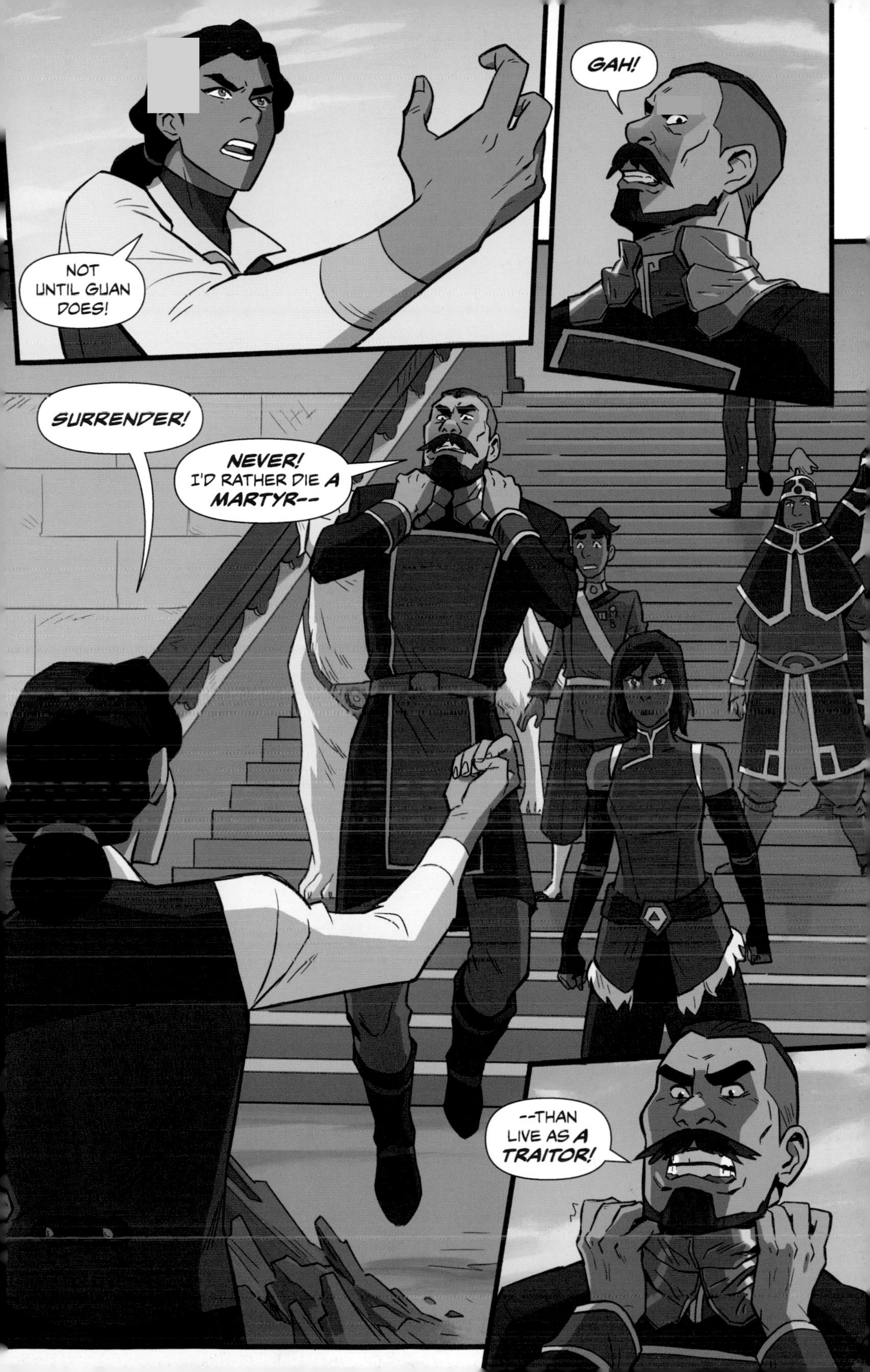
NOT UNTIL GUAN DOES!
GAH!
SURRENDER!
NEVER! I'D RATHER DIE A MARTYR--
--THAN LIVE AS A TRAITOR!

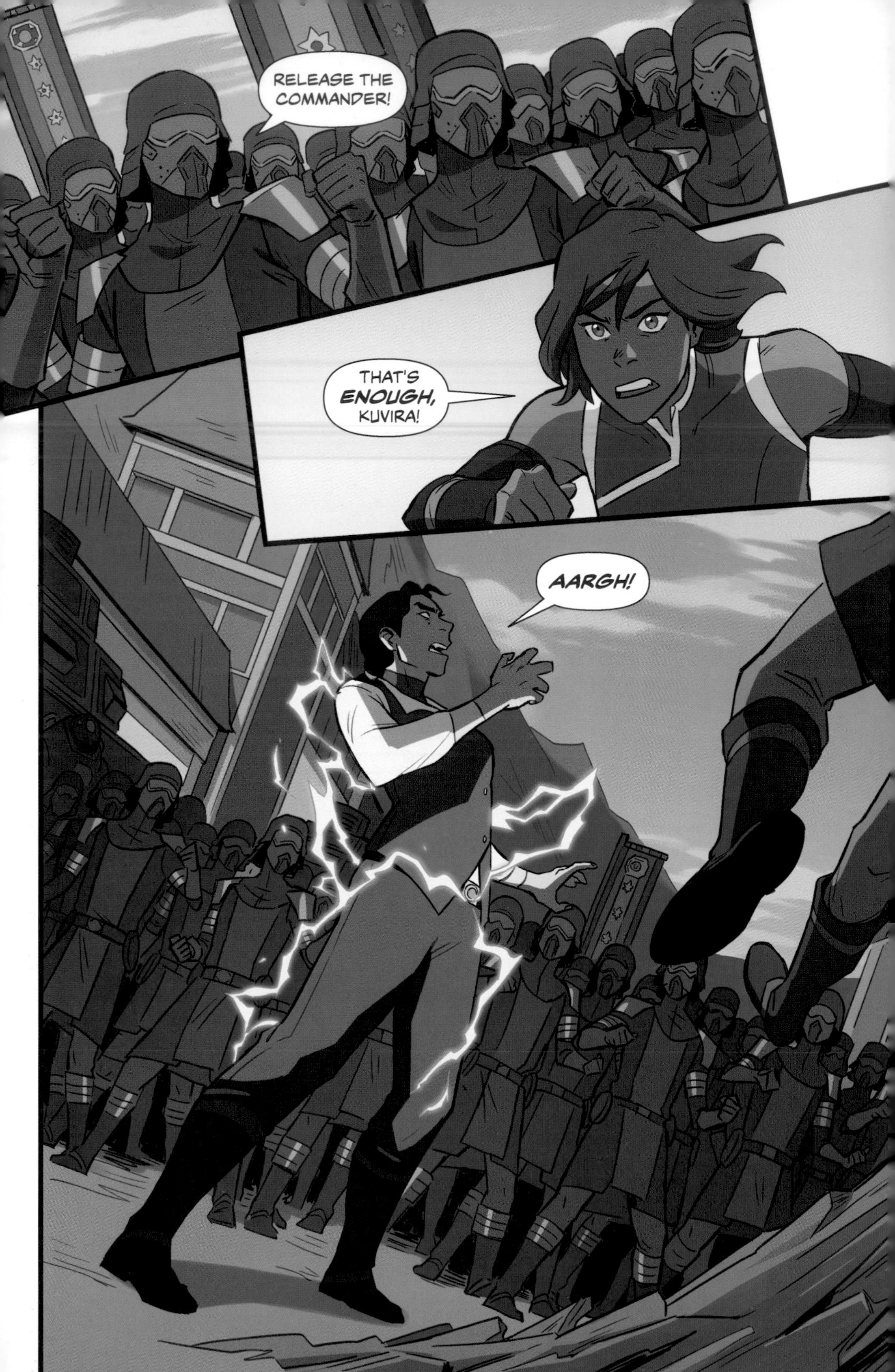
RELEASE THE COMMANDER!
THAT'S ENOUGH, KUVIRA!
AARGH!

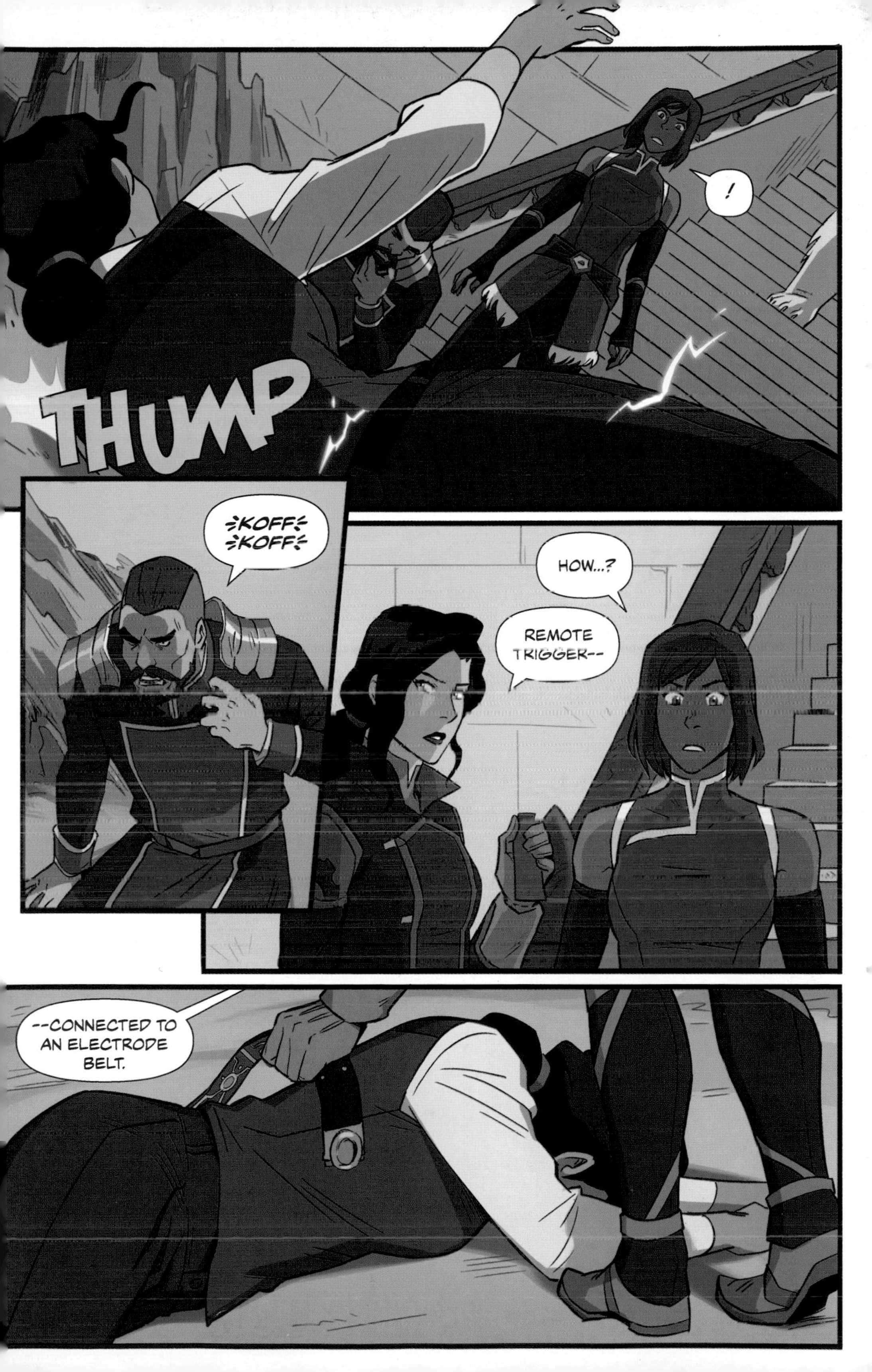

!
THUMP
KOFF KOFF
HOW...?
REMOTE TRIGGER--
--CONNECTED TO AN ELECTRODE BELT.

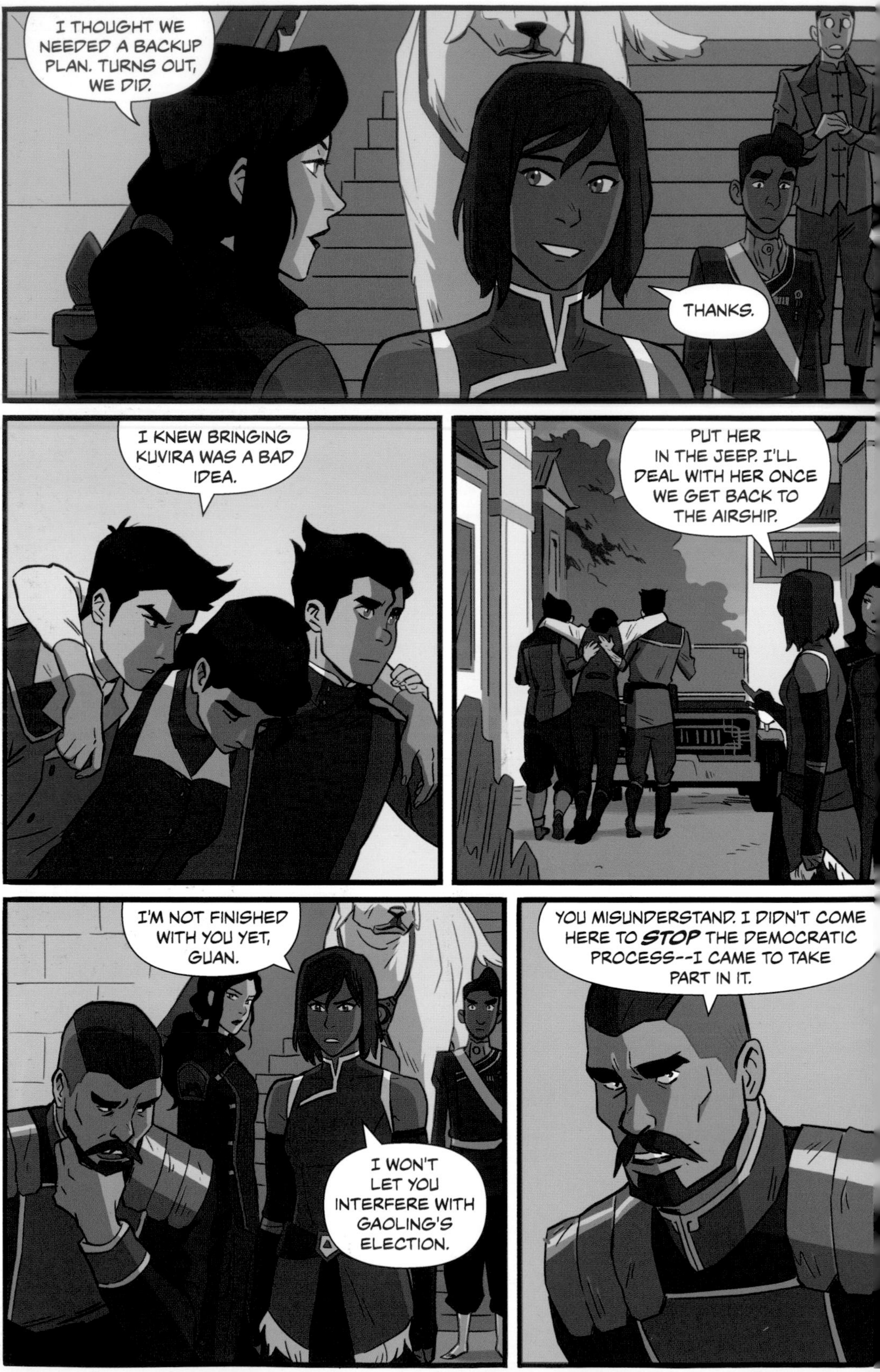
I THOUGHT WE NEEDED A BACKUP PLAN. TURNS OUT, WE DID.
THANKS.
I KNEW BRINGING KUVIRA WAS A BAD IDEA.
PUT HER IN THE JEEP. I'LL DEAL WITH HER ONCE WE GET BACK TO THE AIRSHIP.
I'M NOT FINISHED WITH YOU YET, GUAN.
I WON'T LET YOU INTERFERE WITH GAOLING'S ELECTION.
YOU MISUNDERSTAND. I DIDN'T COME HERE TO STOP THE DEMOCRATIC PROCESS--I CAME TO TAKE PART IN IT.

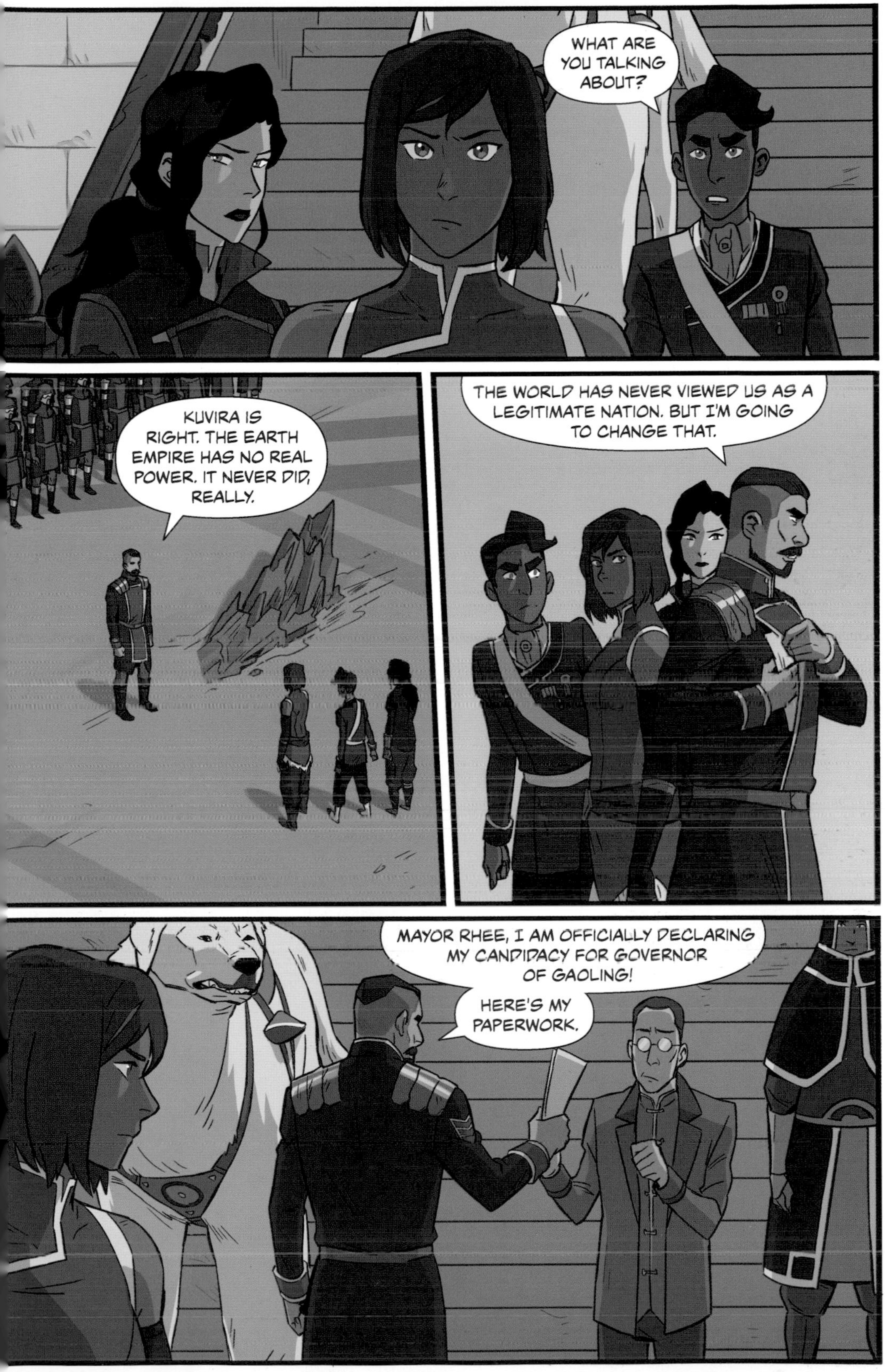
WHAT ARE YOU TALKING ABOUT?
KUVIRA IS RIGHT. THE EARTH EMPIRE HAS NO REAL POWER. IT NEVER DID, REALLY.
THE WORLD HAS NEVER VIEWED US AS A LEGITIMATE NATION. BUT I'M GOING TO CHANGE THAT.
MAYOR RHEE, I AM OFFICIALLY DECLARING MY CANDIDACY FOR GOVERNOR OF GAOLING!
HERE'S MY PAPERWORK.

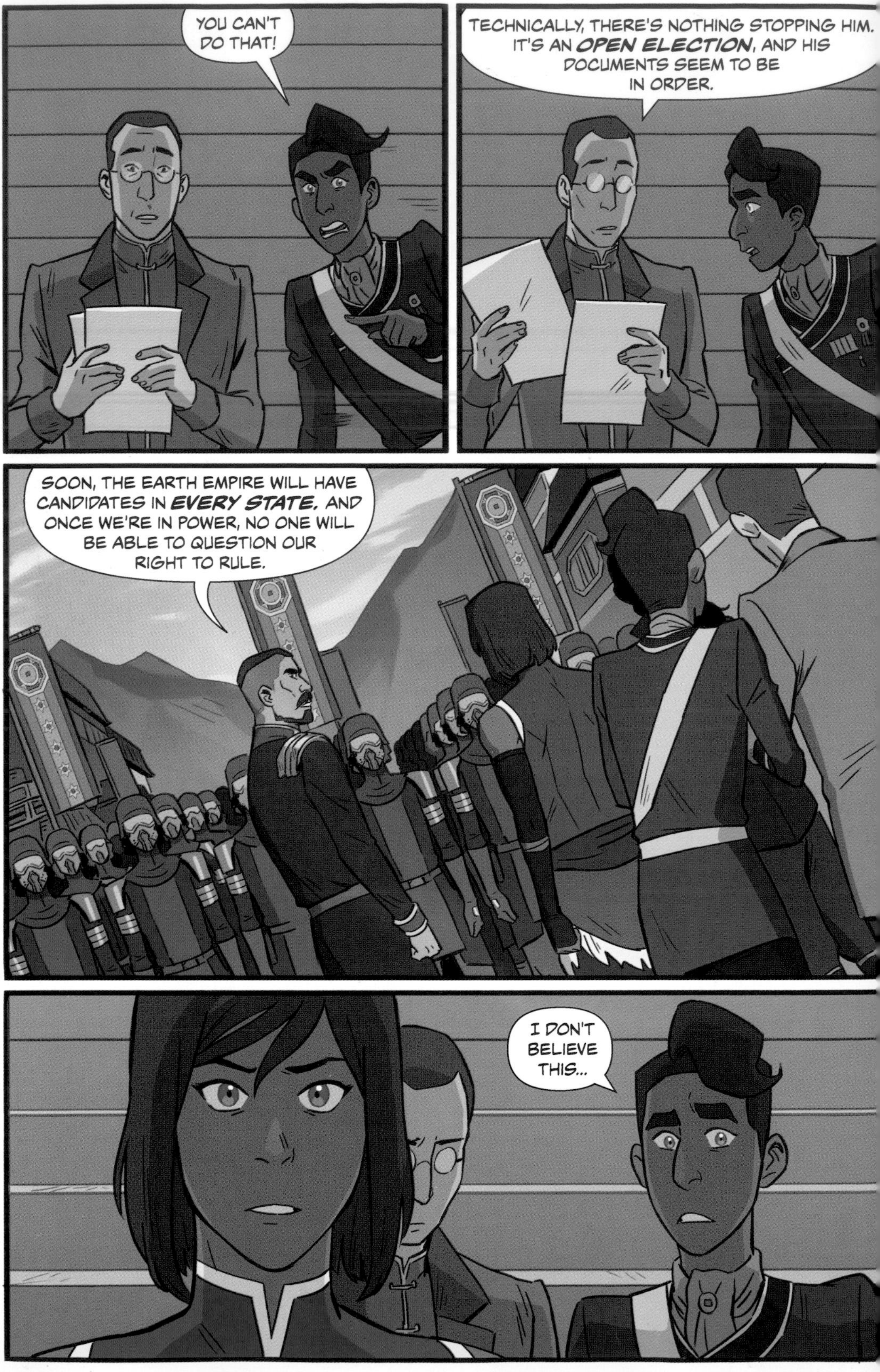
YOU CAN'T DO THAT!
TECHNICALLY, THERE'S NOTHING STOPPING HIM. IT'S AN OPEN ELECTION, AND HIS DOCUMENTS SEEM TO BE IN ORDER.
SOON, THE EARTH EMPIRE WILL HAVE CANDIDATES IN EVERY STATE. AND ONCE WE'RE IN POWER, NO ONE WILL BE ABLE TO QUESTION OUR RIGHT TO RULE.
I DON'T BELIEVE THIS...

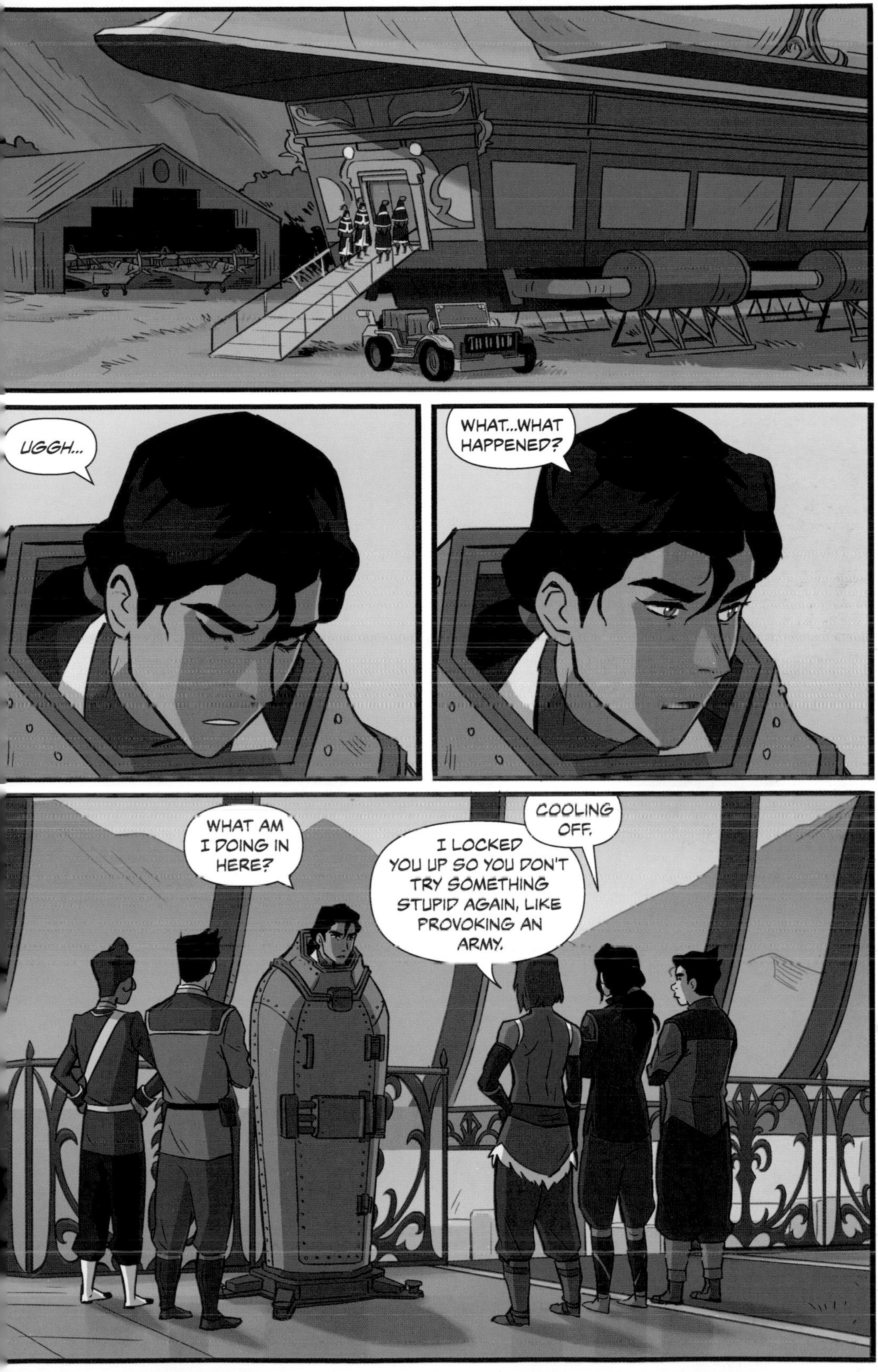
UGGH...
WHAT...WHAT HAPPENED?
WHAT AM I DOING IN HERE?
COOLING OFF.
I LOCKED YOU UP SO YOU DON'T TRY SOMETHING STUPID AGAIN, LIKE PROVOKING AN ARMY.

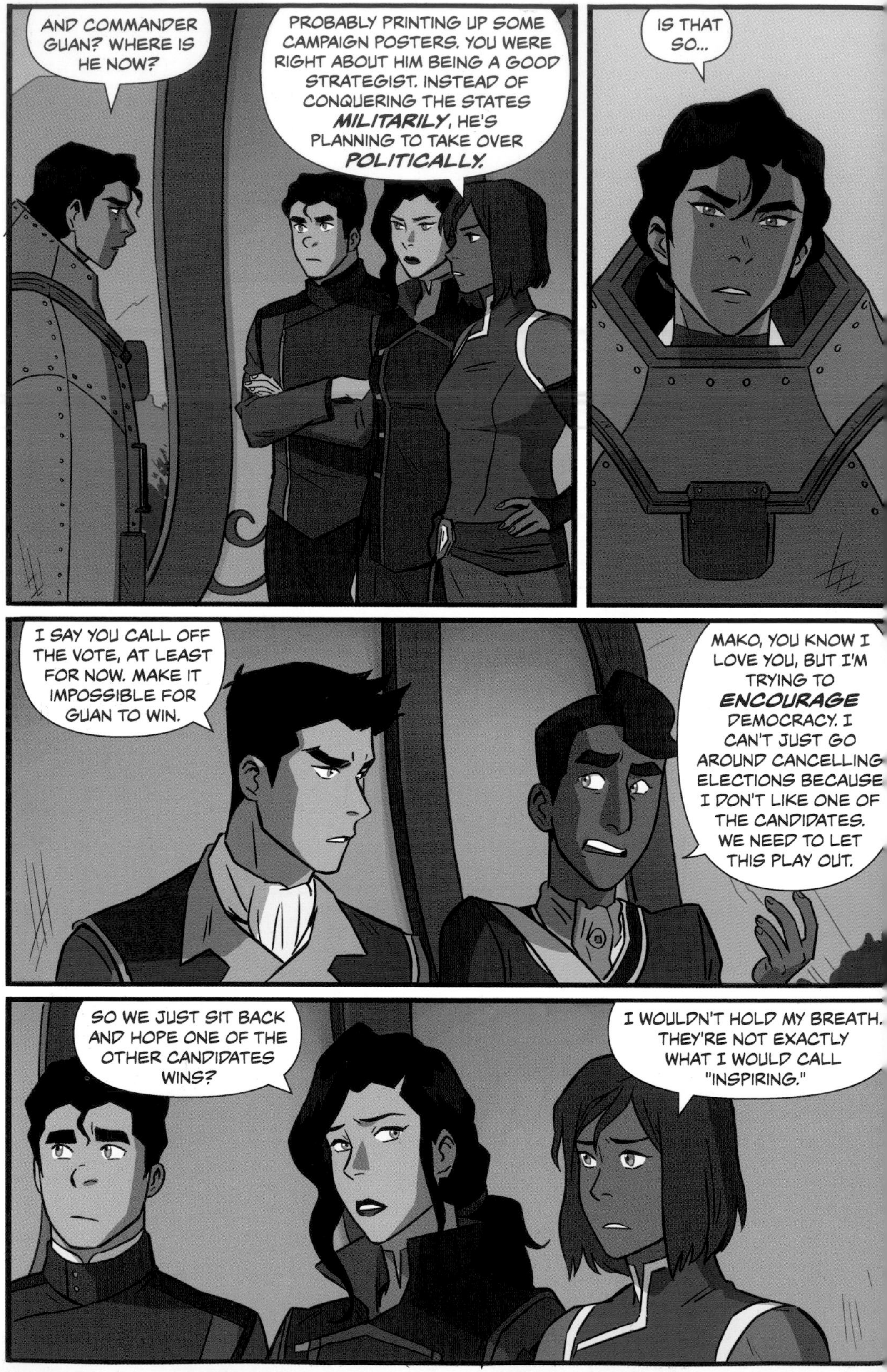
AND COMMANDER GUAN? WHERE IS HE NOW?
PROBABLY PRINTING UP SOME CAMPAIGN POSTERS. YOU WERE RIGHT ABOUT HIM BEING A GOOD STRATEGIST. INSTEAD OF CONQUERING THE STATES *MILITARILY*, HE'S PLANNING TO TAKE OVER *POLITICALLY.*
IS THAT SO...
I SAY YOU CALL OFF THE VOTE, AT LEAST FOR NOW. MAKE IT IMPOSSIBLE FOR GUAN TO WIN.
MAKO, YOU KNOW I LOVE YOU, BUT I'M TRYING TO *ENCOURAGE* DEMOCRACY. I CAN'T JUST GO AROUND CANCELLING ELECTIONS BECAUSE I DON'T LIKE ONE OF THE CANDIDATES. WE NEED TO LET THIS PLAY OUT.
SO WE JUST SIT BACK AND HOPE ONE OF THE OTHER CANDIDATES WINS?
I WOULDN'T HOLD MY BREATH. THEY'RE NOT EXACTLY WHAT I WOULD CALL "INSPIRING."

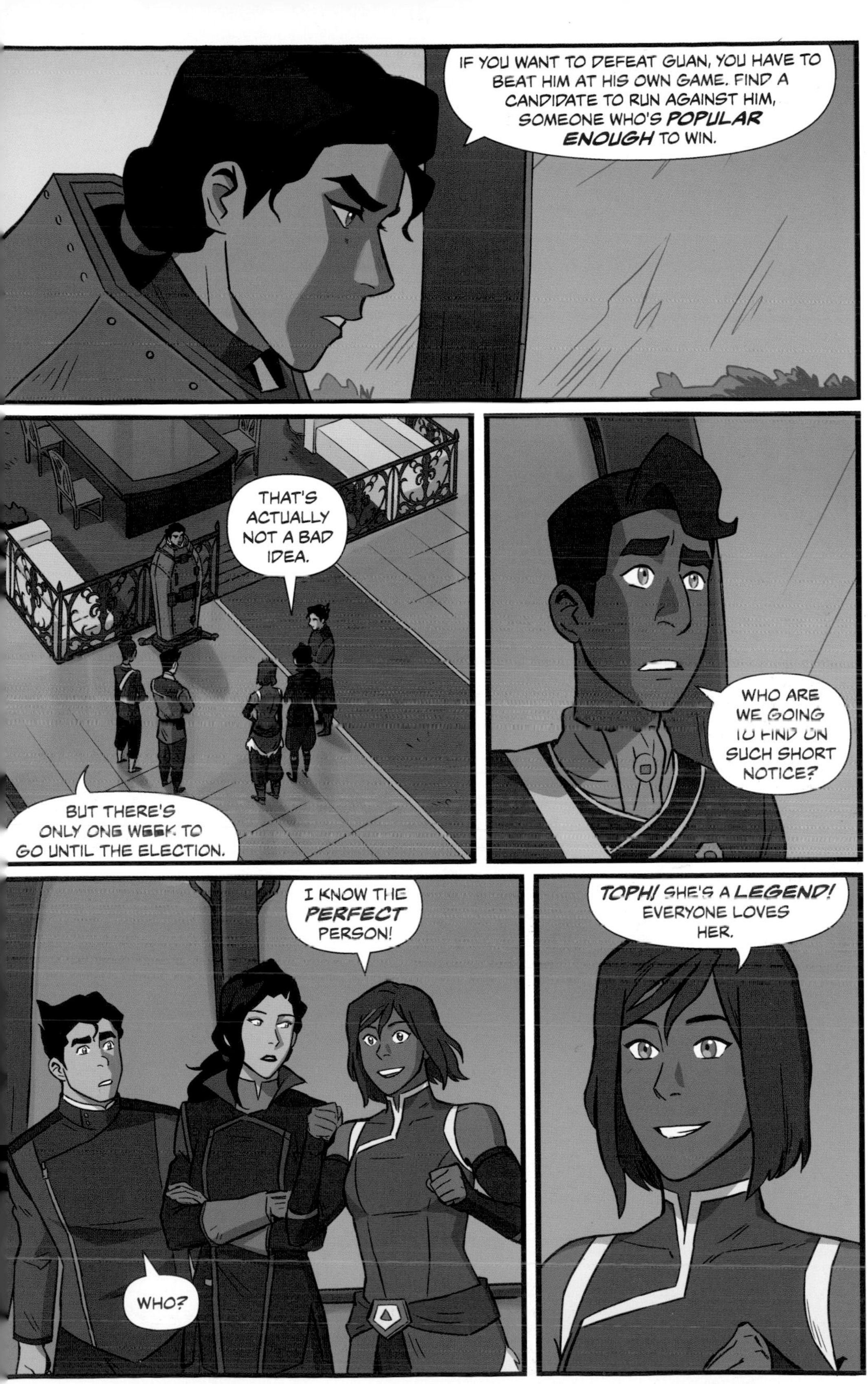

IF YOU WANT TO DEFEAT GUAN, YOU HAVE TO BEAT HIM AT HIS OWN GAME. FIND A CANDIDATE TO RUN AGAINST HIM, SOMEONE WHO'S ***POPULAR ENOUGH*** TO WIN.
THAT'S ACTUALLY NOT A BAD IDEA.
BUT THERE'S ONLY ONE WEEK TO GO UNTIL THE ELECTION.
WHO ARE WE GOING TO FIND ON SUCH SHORT NOTICE?
I KNOW THE ***PERFECT*** PERSON!
WHO?
***TOPH!*** SHE'S A ***LEGEND!*** EVERYONE LOVES HER.

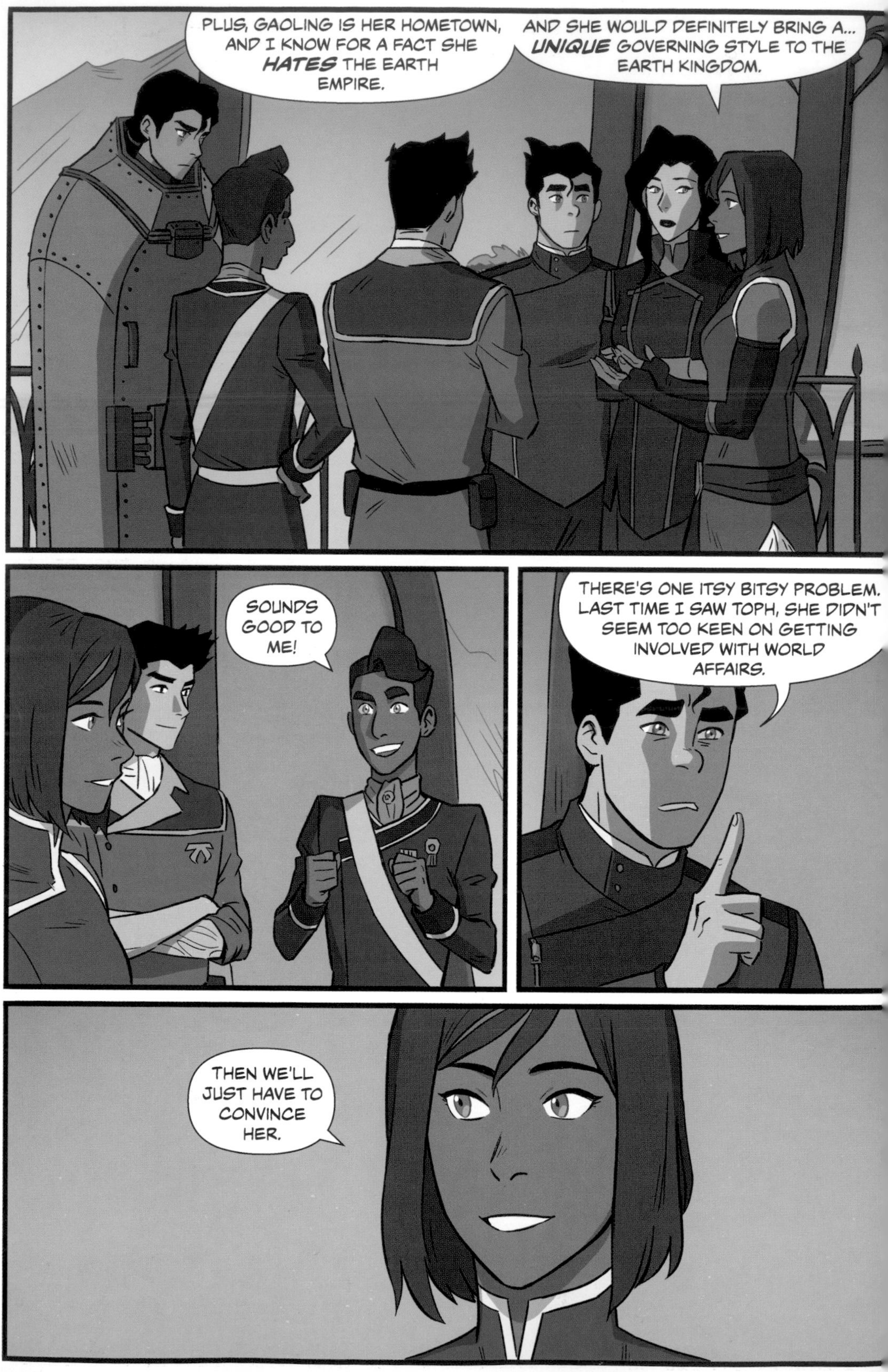
PLUS, GAOLING IS HER HOMETOWN, AND I KNOW FOR A FACT SHE *HATES* THE EARTH EMPIRE.
AND SHE WOULD DEFINITELY BRING A... *UNIQUE* GOVERNING STYLE TO THE EARTH KINGDOM.
SOUNDS GOOD TO ME!
THERE'S ONE ITSY BITSY PROBLEM. LAST TIME I SAW TOPH, SHE DIDN'T SEEM TOO KEEN ON GETTING INVOLVED WITH WORLD AFFAIRS.
THEN WE'LL JUST HAVE TO CONVINCE HER.

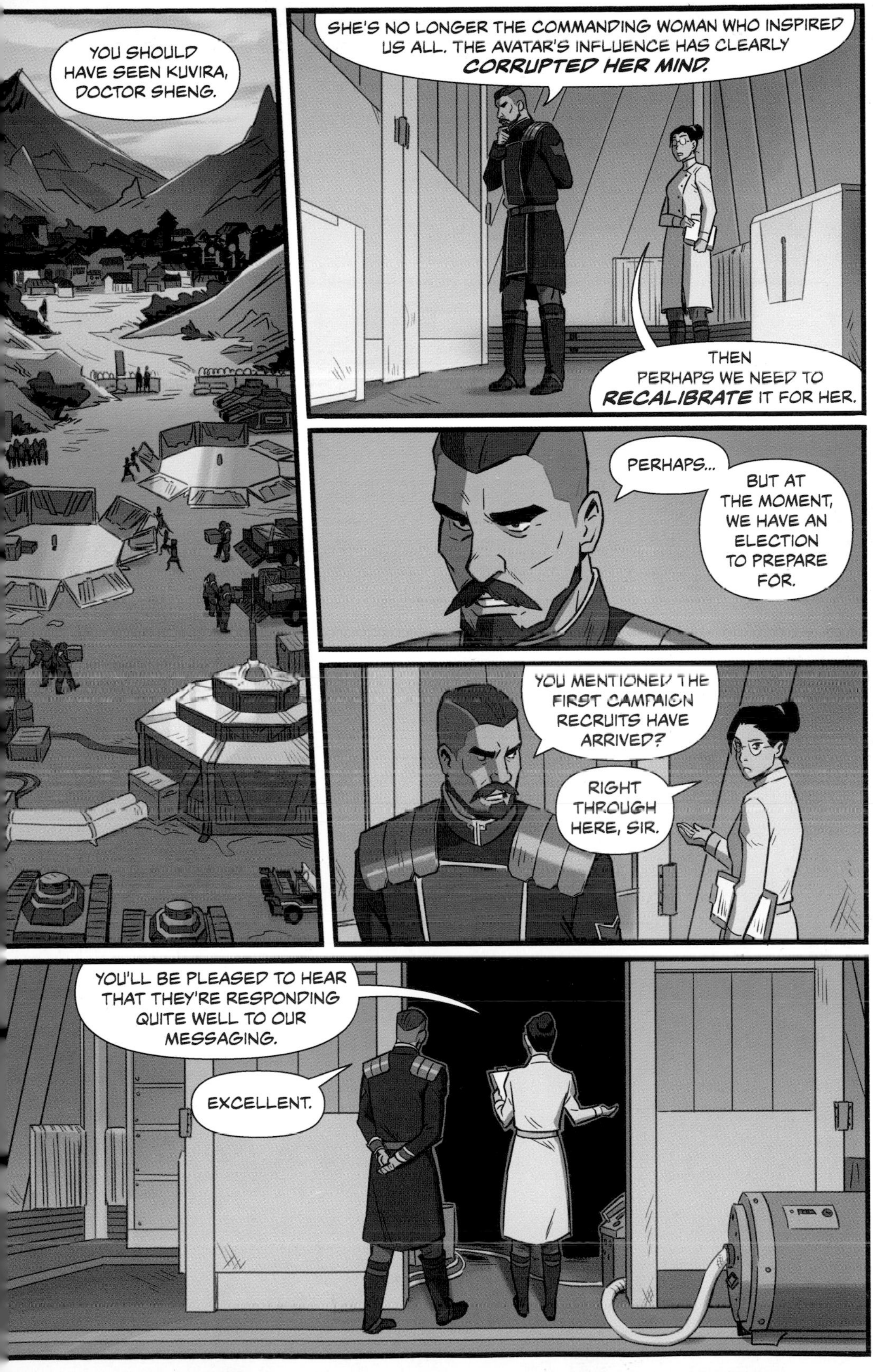
YOU SHOULD HAVE SEEN KUVIRA, DOCTOR SHENG.
SHE'S NO LONGER THE COMMANDING WOMAN WHO INSPIRED US ALL. THE AVATAR'S INFLUENCE HAS CLEARLY CORRUPTED HER MIND.
THEN PERHAPS WE NEED TO RECALIBRATE IT FOR HER.
PERHAPS...
BUT AT THE MOMENT, WE HAVE AN ELECTION TO PREPARE FOR.
YOU MENTIONED THE FIRST CAMPAIGN RECRUITS HAVE ARRIVED?
RIGHT THROUGH HERE, SIR.
YOU'LL BE PLEASED TO HEAR THAT THEY'RE RESPONDING QUITE WELL TO OUR MESSAGING.
EXCELLENT.

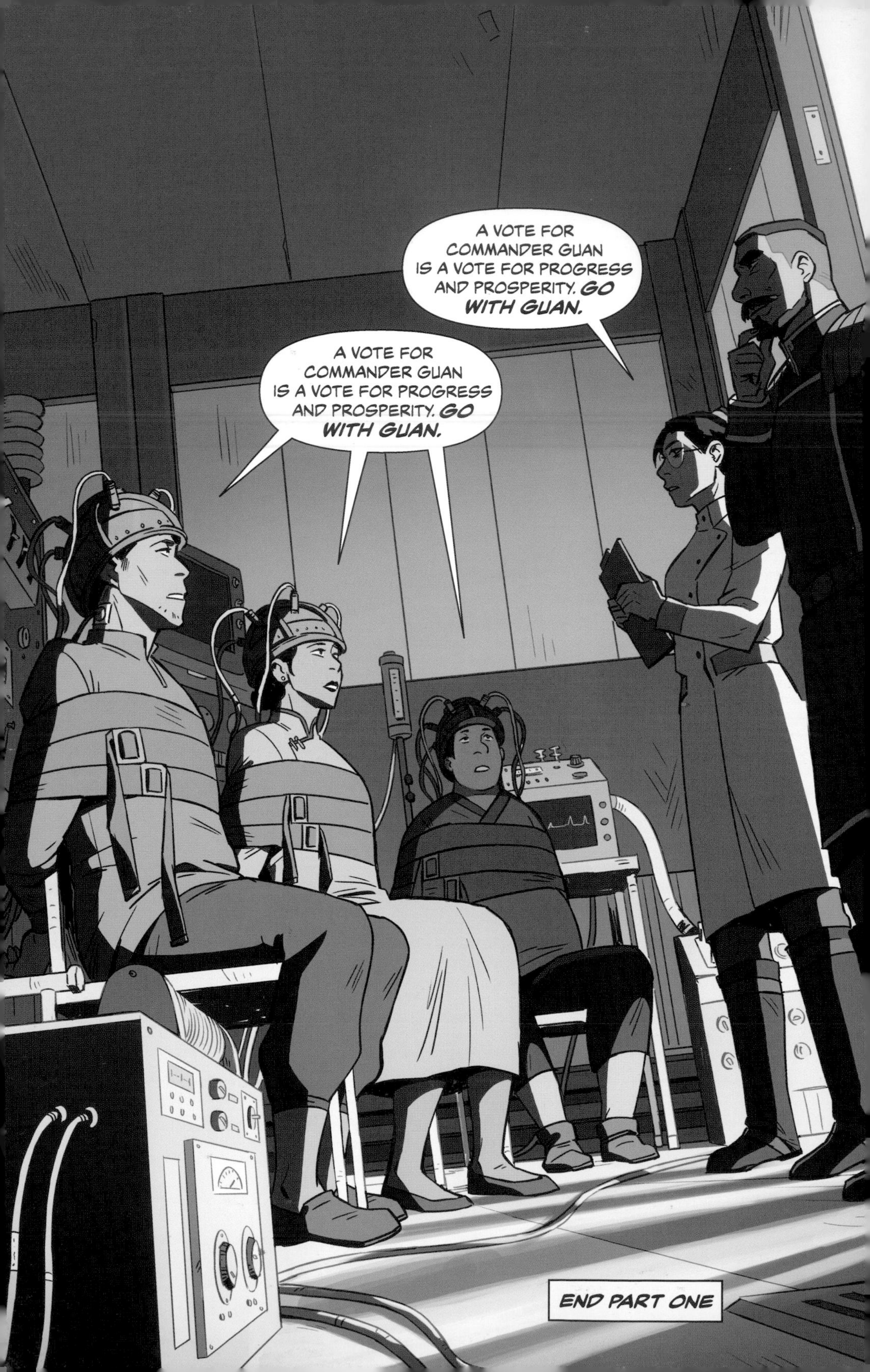
A VOTE FOR COMMANDER GUAN IS A VOTE FOR PROGRESS AND PROSPERITY. GO WITH GUAN.
A VOTE FOR COMMANDER GUAN IS A VOTE FOR PROGRESS AND PROSPERITY. GO WITH GUAN.
END PART ONE

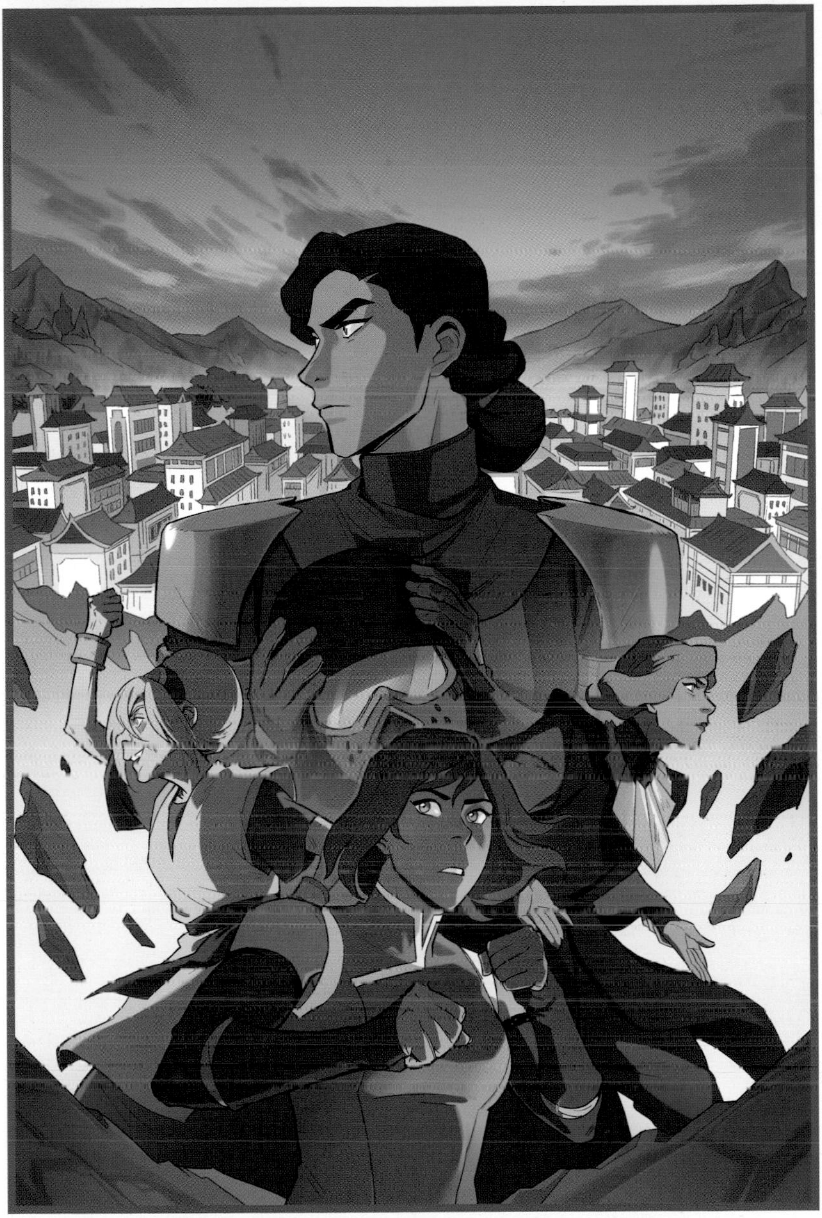

## COMING IN OCTOBER 2019!

The threat to peace in the Earth Kingdom increases . . .

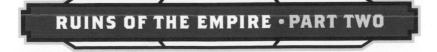

**RUINS OF THE EMPIRE • PART TWO**

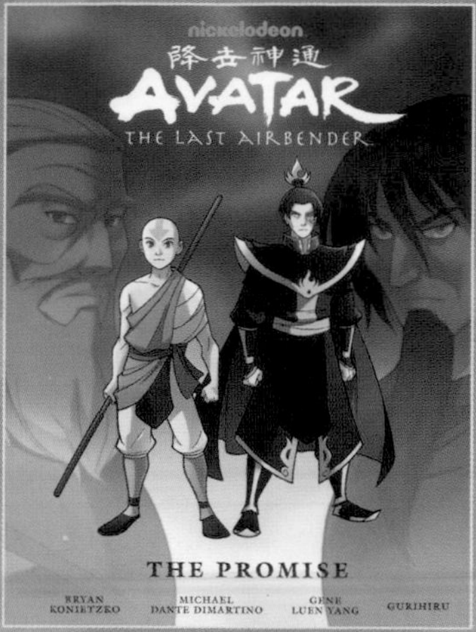
nickelodeon
降去神通
AVATAR
THE LAST AIRBENDER
THE PROMISE
BRYAN KONIETZKO
MICHAEL DANTE DIMARTINO
GENE LUEN YANG
GURIHIRU

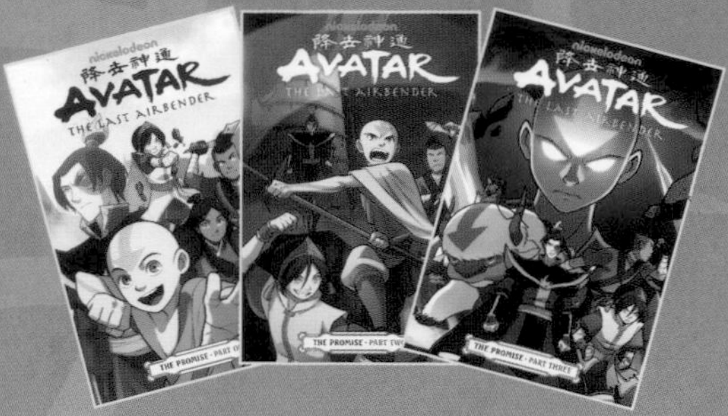

**Avatar: The Last Airbender—The Promise Library Edition**
978-1-61655-074-5 $39.99

**Avatar: The Last Airbender—The Promise Part 1**
978-1-59582-811-8 $10.99

**Avatar: The Last Airbender—The Promise Part 2**
978-1-59582-875-0 $10.99

**Avatar: The Last Airbender—The Promise Part 3**
978-1-59582-941-2 $10.99

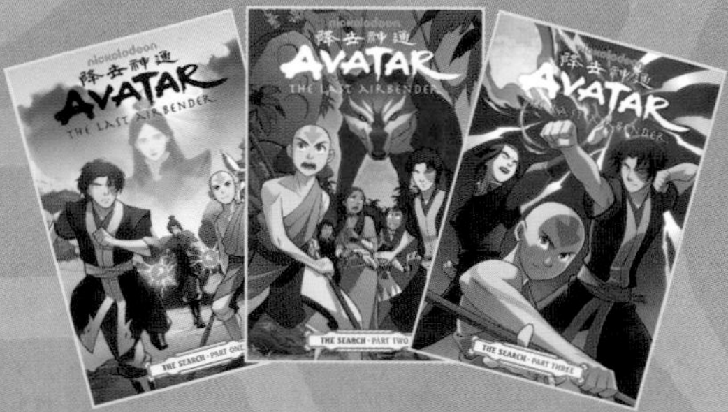

**Avatar: The Last Airbender—The Search Library Edition**
978-1-61655-226-8 $39.99

**Avatar: The Last Airbender—The Search Part 1**
978-1-61655-054-7 $10.99

**Avatar: The Last Airbender—The Search Part 2**
978-1-61655-190-2 $10.99

**Avatar: The Last Airbender—The Search Part 3**
978-1-61655-184-1 $10.99

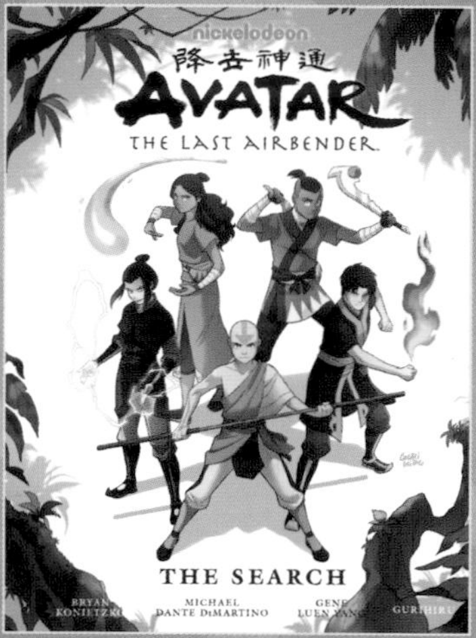
nickelodeon
降去神通
AVATAR
THE LAST AIRBENDER
THE SEARCH
MICHAEL DANTE DIMARTINO
GURIHIRU

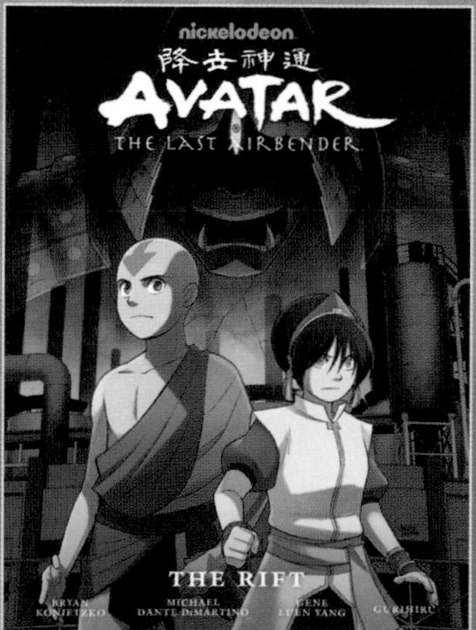
nickelodeon
降去神通
AVATAR
THE LAST AIRBENDER
THE RIFT
BRYAN KONIETZKO
MICHAEL DANTE DIMARTINO
GENE LUEN YANG
GURIHIRU

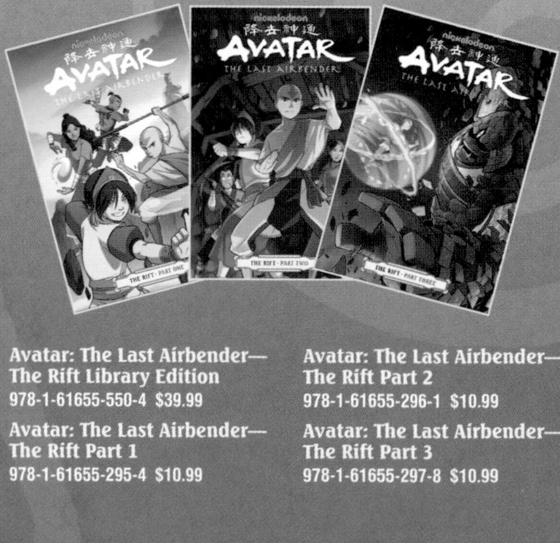

**Avatar: The Last Airbender—The Rift Library Edition**
978-1-61655-550-4 $39.99

**Avatar: The Last Airbender—The Rift Part 1**
978-1-61655-295-4 $10.99

**Avatar: The Last Airbender—The Rift Part 2**
978-1-61655-296-1 $10.99

**Avatar: The Last Airbender—The Rift Part 3**
978-1-61655-297-8 $10.99

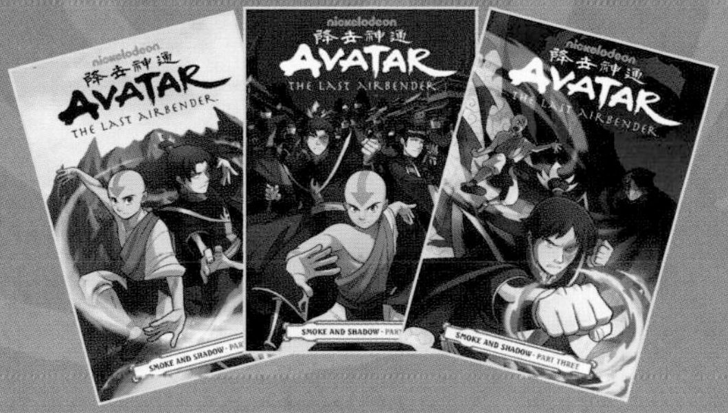

**Avatar: The Last Airbender—Smoke and Shadow Library Edition**
978-1-50670-013-7 $39.99

**Avatar: The Last Airbender—Smoke and Shadow Part 1**
978-1-61655-761-4 $10.99

**Avatar: The Last Airbender—Smoke and Shadow Part 2**
978-1-61655-790-4 $10.99

**Avatar: The Last Airbender—Smoke and Shadow Part 3**
978-1-61655-838-3 $10.99

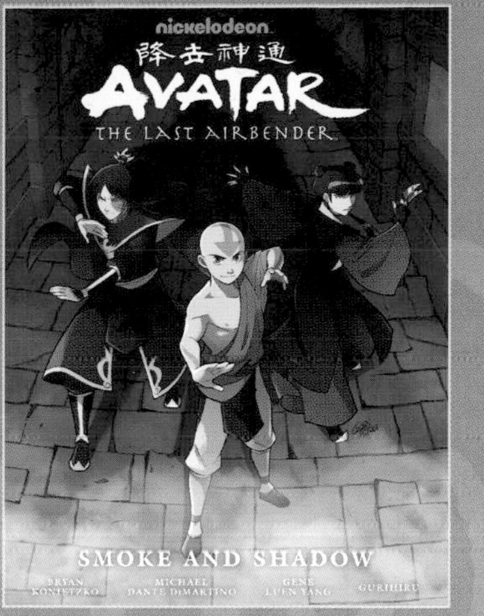
nickelodeon
降去神通
AVATAR
THE LAST AIRBENDER
SMOKE AND SHADOW
BRYAN KONIETZKO
MICHAEL DANTE DiMARTINO
GENE LUEN YANG
GURIHIRU

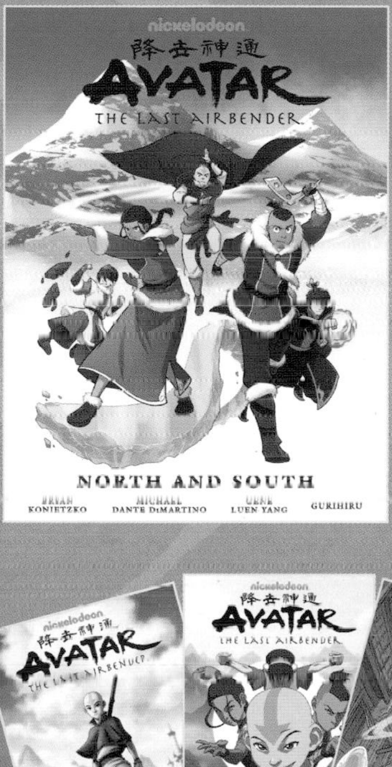
nickelodeon
降去神通
AVATAR
THE LAST AIRBENDER
NORTH AND SOUTH
BRYAN KONIETZKO
MICHAEL DANTE DiMARTINO
GENE LUEN YANG
GURIHIRU

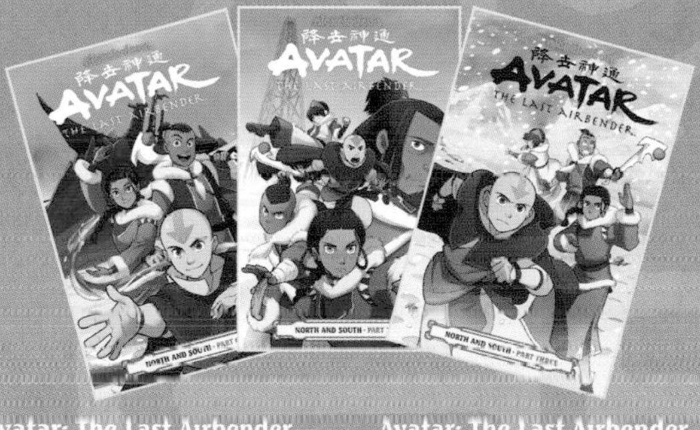

**Avatar: The Last Airbender—North and South Part 1**
978-1-50670-022-9 $10.99

**Avatar: The Last Airbender—North and South Part 2**
978-1-50670-129-5 $10.99

**Avatar: The Last Airbender—North and South Part 3**
978-1-50670-130-1 $10.99

**Avatar: The Last Airbender—North And South Library Edition**
978-1-50670-195-0 $39.99

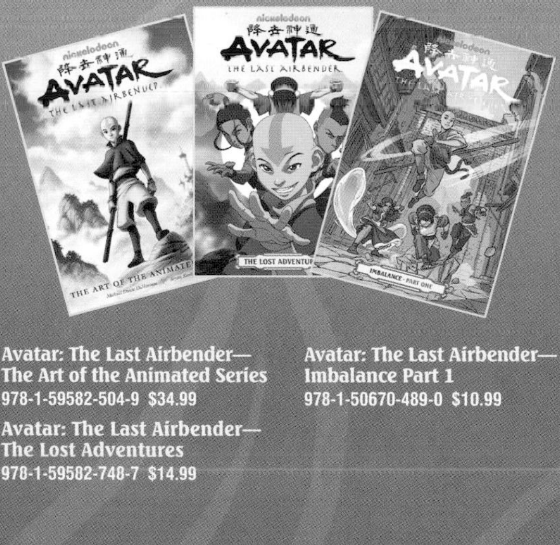

**Avatar: The Last Airbender—The Art of the Animated Series**
978-1-59582-504-9 $34.99

**Avatar: The Last Airbender—The Lost Adventures**
978-1-59582-748-7 $14.99

**Avatar: The Last Airbender—Imbalance Part 1**
978-1-50670-489-0 $10.99

nickelodeon
降去神通
AVATAR
THE LAST AIRBENDER

## BE PART OF THE INCREDIBLE JOURNEY!

**Check out the best-selling graphic novels by acclaimed writer Gene Luen Yang.**

AVAILABLE AT YOUR LOCAL COMICS SHOP OR BOOKSTORE! To find a comics shop in your area, visit comicshoplocator.com. For more information or to order direct visit DarkHorswe.com or call 1-800-862-0052



DARK HORSE BOOKS

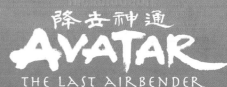

GO BEHIND THE SCENES of the follow-up to the smash-hit series *Avatar: The Last Airbender!* Each volume features hundreds of pieces of never-before-seen artwork created during the development of *The Legend of Korra*. With captions from creators Michael Dante DiMartino and Bryan Konietzko throughout, this is an intimate look inside the creative process that brought the mystical world of bending and a new generation of heroes to life!

**nickelodeon**

# THE LEGEND OF KORRA™

## THE ART OF THE ANIMATED SERIES

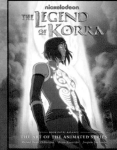

**BOOK ONE: AIR**
978-1-61655-168-1 | $34.99

**BOOK TWO: SPIRITS**
978-1-61655-462-0 | $34.99

**BOOK THREE: CHANGE**
978-1-61655-565-8 | $34.99

**BOOK FOUR: BALANCE**
978-1-61655-687-7 | $34.99